31
WAYS

to be

A "One Another" Christian

loving others with the love of Jesus

When you become a Christian, God puts you, as one of his children, in a relationship with other brothers and sisters. In the pages that follow, you are urged to follow the "one another" commands of the New Testament. But please remember one thing: only if you are truly regenerate—if you have been born again by a gracious work of the Holy Spirit and have come in repentance to God and faith in Christ—will you be able to be a "one another" Christian.

31 WAYS

to be

A "One Another" Christian

loving others with the love of Jesus

Dr. Stuart Scott

~ with S. Andrew Jin ~

The longer I walk with the Lord, pastoring a church and reading my Bible year after year, the more I'm struck by the centrality of love—and not just any kind of love, but street-level love that has feet and that steps into the lives of other people in practical and Christlike ways. So much has been said about the local church lately, but perhaps the greatest need today is for people in church to learn how to love one another, and then to push outside their walls to love broken people around them. This little book will help us get traction on what it really means to love like God has called us to love. Get it. Read it. Put it into practice.

Brad Bigney, Lead Pastor of Grace Fellowship Church, Florence, Kentucky; ACBC Certified Counselor, Conference Speaker, Author of "Gospel Treason—Betraying the Gospel with Hidden Idols"

Dr. Scott and Andrew Jin offer wise insight into the biblical "one another" commands. They carefully explain each text in its context while drawing upon their years of pastoral counseling experience to help the reader make practical applications. This book would be excellent as a daily devotion for an individual or a family. I also believe that it would be very helpful in a discipleship group which needs to better understand and apply the "one another" passages.

Dr. Jim Newheiser, Director of the Christian Counseling Program and Associate Professor of Pastoral Theology, Reformed Theological Seminary Charlotte; Executive Director, The Institute for Biblical Counseling and Discipleship (IBCD)

This is one of the most helpful books to come along in a long time. This instrument in the hands of a Biblical counselor is invaluable to encourage and challenge our counselees to see what God's Word has to say about good relationships. Our society and human nature teach us to be self focused but this handy little book will be a treasure to have as a vehicle for sanctification. I have wanted something like this for a long time and now I will have this tool in my counseling ministry. Not only is the truth of God's Word explained but application is illustrated. God's people will be better off for this work and I commend Stuart Scott and Andrew Jin for bringing it to God's people. Thank you for your labors in God's ministry.

Dr. Bill Shannon, Pastor of Discipleship Counseling, Grace Community Church, Sun Valley, California

In Biblical Counseling, we are frequently tasked with helping people understand how to "do" relationships. Enter this concise, insightful, and entirely practical book by Stuart Scott and Andrew Jin. With explanation, illustration and application of each "one another" passage, Stuart and Andrew lay out how love for God is to be fleshed out in love for others. I'm so very thankful for this excellent resource and will make regular use of it!

Pamela Gannon, RN, MABC, ACBC Certified; Adjunct Professor at Montana Bible College, Co-author of "In The Aftermath: Past the Pain of Childhood Sexual Abuse"

God assesses the maturity of an individual and of churches by the quality of their "one-anothering." In these thirty-one devotionals, Stuart Scott and Andrew Jin "one-another" their readers by unpacking the meaning of key "one another" New Testament passages, illustrating them, and then encouraging the reader to apply the truth to daily living. I recommend this study for individuals, family devotions, small groups, and one-on-one discipleship opportunities.

Dr. Jim Berg, Author of "Changed Into His Image"; Professor of Biblical Counseling, BJU Seminary, Greenville, South Carolina

The so-called "one anothers" of the New Testament are often undervalued and therefore greatly unappreciated by countless numbers of professing Christians. Just ask a relatively mature believer to define—let alone illustrate and apply—the various New Testament passages in which the "one anothers" appear, and you will undoubtedly be found disappointed by their response. Therefore, with a brief definition, then an illustration, and finally an application of these various "one anothers," Stuart Scott, along with co-author Andrew Jin, will encourage you to live out these truths, not merely for your own good, but also for the good of others. And isn't this precisely what living the Christian life is all about—loving your God and your neighbor? Upon these two truths hang all the Law and Prophets of the Old Testament, as Jesus himself declared! What better way to understand "one anothers" in the context of helping us to take God's Word at face value for the purpose of helping ourselves and then our nearest neighbors to honor God as God. So, take up and read this little book and learn how to minister to one another in the fear of God.

Dr. Lance Quinn, Senior Pastor, Bethany Bible Church, Thousand Oaks, California

This book is an excellent idea! It is convicting and very practical. I highly recommend it to those who will read it thoughtfully "looking to themselves" to obey God's commands of one-anothering.
Martha Peace, Author of "The Excellent Wife" and Certified Biblical Counselor with ACBC

It can be easy as a writer to give instruction without talking about how to implement that instruction, making it easy as a reader to fail to put good instruction into practice. Stuart and Andrew have worked hard to help us avoid that trap. So, as you read their book, look forward to lots of helpful instruction *and* lots of direction for how to apply the instruction. I'm confident that as we put these truths into practice our relationships and our churches will profit.
Dr. Amy Baker, Biblical Counselor and Ministry Resource Director at Faith Church, Lafayette, Indiana

Dr. Scott, author of *From Pride to Humility,* has done it again in writing an excellent resource for all Christians. Not only does he challenge the reader regarding the "one another" biblical commands, but he also assists the reader with understanding the meaning behind those commands in context, offering biblical, practical help. This resource will greatly enhance my own walk with Christ, and those I counsel. Get it and be blessed by it!
Dr. Shelbi Cullen, ACBC Certified, Adjunct Professor of Biblical Counseling and Studies at The Master's University, Santa Clarita, California

Utilizing the "one anothers" of the New Testament, Dr. Scott and Andrew Jin provide a template to biblically evaluate our personal walk with Christ. They also provide clear explanations for straightforward action steps that will encourage believers to grow in maturity. The trifold aim of killing sin, pursuing holiness, and growing in fellowship with others will benefit all who engage the authors' wise counsel.
Dr. T. Dale Johnson, Jr., Executive Director, The Association of Certified Biblical Counselors; Associate Professor of Biblical Counseling, Midwestern Baptist Theological Seminary

I love how this book is both thoroughly biblical but also immensely practical. The chapters are very brief and to the point and therefore ideal for small group Bible studies or counseling assignments. All our churches would do well to study this material and ask our risen Lord to help us put these principles into greater practice in his church.

Dr. Steve Viars, Senior Pastor, Faith Baptist Church, Lafayette, Indiana

Recognizing that Christian maturity requires and reflects loving relationships, Scott and Jin provide brief but thoughtful reflections on the expansive array of New Testament "one another" commands. The short segments and the practical—and at times, searching—applications make it a helpful guide for personal devotions, counseling homework, adult class study, or small group discussion.

Robert D. Jones, D.Theol., D.Min., Biblical Counseling Professor at The Southern Baptist Theological Seminary; Author of "Uprooting Anger and Pursuing Peace"

It is virtually impossible to overestimate the contribution that loving, truthful, "one another" relationships will bring to the progress of disciple-making in our local churches. To that end, Stuart Scott and Andrew Jin have given the church gracious, heart-challenging counsel to help us grow toward maturity in Christ.

Dr. Paul Tautges, Author; Senior Pastor, Cornerstone Community Church, Mayfield Heights, Ohio; Founder, Counseling One Another

Stuart Scott is more serious and more careful than anyone I have ever met when it comes to understanding the text of Scripture and applying it to life. This book is the overflow of wisdom from a man who has carefully studied the Bible, worked carefully to live it out in his own life, and, with Andrew Jin, now wants to share the fruit with you. For those who love Jesus, there isn't a better goal than to grow in the faithfulness of living in Christian community. And for anyone who has that goal, they could not have a better teacher than Stuart Scott. I can't wait to see what happens in your life and in your church as God adds his blessing to your study of this book.

Dr. Heath Lambert, Senior Pastor, First Baptist Church of Jacksonville, Florida

© 2019 Stuart Scott and S. Andrew Jin

ISBN
Paper: 978-1-63342-176-9
epub: 978-1-63342-177-6
Kindle: 978-1-63342-178-3

Shepherd Press
P.O. Box 24
Wapwallopen, PA 18660
www.shepherdpress.com

Book Design and Cover by www.greatwriting.org

Table of Contents

Introduction: A Word About Relationships

People, created in the image of God, are made for relationships. Although the term "relationship" does not appear as a word in most modern translations of the Bible, the concept is found in all the books of the Bible. The term "one another" is repeated numerous times in the New Testament—and always in a way that demonstrates how one believer is to relate (or be in a certain relationship) to another believer.

Because sin entered the world, the way people relate to one another is often disrupted. The breakdown of relationships is apparent in the home, in the church, and in society all around. Many people go to pastors or counselors for guidance because of problems they have in their relationships with others—problems with their spouses, children, parents, siblings, friends, coworkers, employers, employees, etc.

The good news is that the Bible has a lot to say about how to build God-honoring relationships with one another. It all starts with God, and your love for him—something that begins when you come to repentance and faith—when you experience the new birth and become a believer in Jesus. Jesus made this point very clearly in what he taught about the first and greatest commandment, a passage recorded in Matthew 22:36-40:

> "Teacher, which is the great commandment in the Law?" And he said to him, "You shall love the Lord your God with all your heart and with all your soul and with all your mind. This is the great and first commandment. And a second is like it: You shall love your neighbor as yourself. On these two commandments depend all the Law and the Prophets."

From this passage, it is abundantly clear that God intends you to be consciously and carefully loving him and other people. Your relationship with God and your relationship with others is directly and intricately linked. As you work on loving other believers by obeying the "one another" commands, you are, in fact, also growing in your love for God.

The "one another" passages of Scripture give very clear guidance on how to develop and maintain good relationships. As you work your way through the various passages in the New Testament, you will find that you are not only being built up in your faith, but you will have the wonderful effect of building up others in their faith, too! So, whether you use this book by yourself, with a friend or marriage partner, or in a small or larger group, you will find much to put into practice.

1

Be Devoted to One Another with Brotherly Love

"Love one another with brotherly affection."

Romans 12:10a

EXPLANATION

This command is to treat other believers as you would treat a family member. If you get along well with your brothers and sisters, you know what this means. Some readers have not experienced loving, heartfelt sibling relationships. Even so, you can still look to Scripture to give proper guidance.

What kinds of feelings are associated with a family? One would expect warmth, concern, care, and devotion. Romans 12:10 specifically states that one is to love one another with brotherly affection. "Brotherly affection" is the translation of the Greek word "philadelphia" which means "love of the brethren." This term denotes a tender and strong affection[1] for one's family members. Why does Paul use a term that is traditionally associated with family—that is, blood relatives—to show how believers should treat one another? Because most people are devoted first and foremost to their blood relatives before they are to others. However, God calls believers to have a devotion to other believers that is the same as one's devotion to immediate family members. Christians are members of one another—all being a part of the family of Jesus Christ. Romans 12:5 states it well: "So we, though many, are one body in Christ, and individually members one of another." Believers should be so devoted to one another that they do good first and foremost to those who are of the "household of faith" (Galatians 6:10).

ILLUSTRATION

When we go to church and see all the different people, we tend to go to or talk to folks with whom we already feel comfortable. These people are friends or small-group members or those we meet in Bible study. But as we look at the congregation, we should start to see them as blood relatives and show affection accordingly. Think of your family gathering at Christmas Day or Thanksgiving. You are not just sitting around asking, "How are you?" and replying, "Fine." No, you want to know what has been happening in their lives during the past year. You are genuinely curious and sincere as you talk with brothers and sisters, mothers and fathers. This is how you are to be with other believers.

APPLICATION

» *How can you work toward being much more intentional in showing brotherly affection to other believers?*

» *List several good things from your relationship with family members you can implement in your relationship with other believers.*

» *Write down the name of one believer you have been neglecting to treat like a blood relative. Then mention several specific ways you can implement this command in your life this week.*

2

Outdo One Another in Showing Honor

"Outdo one another in showing honor."

Romans 12:10b

EXPLANATION

Paul gives this command to outdo one another shortly after he has urged readers to "present your bodies as a living sacrifice, holy and acceptable to God, which is your spiritual worship" (Romans 12:1). Proper love for and worship of God is linked to proper love for and treatment of other believers.

What does it mean to honor? Honor means to give special weight or value to the other person. So outdoing one another in showing honor means giving the other person weighty, serious consideration in all things.

Notice that the command is to outdo, not to give honor. Honor is the manner in which one is to outdo. We are to praise, recognize, and show special attention to the other person more than we would receive from him or her. We must "outdo" the other person.

Illustration

"Hi, how are you?" "I'm fine, thanks; how are you?" This is the standard greeting that we use. When we meet another person, it's not long until we tend toward talking (or wanting to talk) about ourselves more than we want to take an interest in the other person. This "one another" places ourselves in a humble posture and lifts the other person up in our viewpoint. We should be saying to ourselves, "This person is of more importance than I am." This will help us to love him or her and truly take an interest in such a person above ourselves.

Application

» *Are you consciously seeking to prefer others over yourself? For example, when you are in a conversation, do you dominate the conversation? Is the topic often about you? If so, you are not outdoing the other person in showing honor. Think about the last conversation you had with another believer. How could you have thought more and cared more about the other person?*

» *List one believer you can prefer with honor. How can you make the other person "weigh heavy" in your life this week? How can you value that person? List three specific ways you can do this and be specific, stating both how and when you will do it.*

3

Live in Harmony with One Another

"Live in harmony with one another. Do not be haughty, but associate with the lowly. Never be wise in your own sight."

Romans 12:16

EXPLANATION

Living in harmony with one another involves having the same mind as the other person in one's thinking. It means to agree or to have a common mind. Now, having a common mind does not mean that a believer must think exactly the same thoughts as another believer or think exactly the same way about everything—that would be impossible and absurd. Rather, believers are to have the same kind of thinking about one another. For example, they are to think well of one another, seek to love one another, bring encouragement to one another, etc. God is calling believers, regardless of their social, economic, or ethnic status[2] to "have equal regard for one another."[3]

What is the barrier to living in harmony with one another? Simply put, it is pride. This "one another" command goes against pride. Pride seeks to make a person think more highly of himself than he ought to think. Just a few verses before this "one another" command (Romans 12:3), Paul states this very same thing. If one is proud, he or she will think highly of self—and this necessarily means thinking of others as being more lowly. Romans 12:16 contrasts the "haughty" thinking with "lowly" thinking. The end of verse 16 states, "Never be wise in your own sight." The same thought is found in Proverbs 3:6-7: "In all your ways acknowledge him, and he will make straight your paths. Be not wise in your own eyes; fear the Lord, and turn away from evil." This section in Proverbs is about trusting in God and not relying on one's own lofty thinking.

Practically speaking, there is to be no social or intellectual aristocracy[4] in the church. There should be no vain ambition, no fighting for position. People should have the same mind toward one another.

Illustration

"Let me play the devil's advocate." Have you heard this before? Well, we should not want to take that posture according to this "one another" teaching. Instead, we should seek to agree wherever we can. We should be seeking unity in God's truth. The church should be striving for a like-mindedness rather than an argumentative or divisive attitude.

» *How and when do you find yourself thinking
  more highly of yourself than you ought?*

» *Do you notice a particular pattern in your
  thinking toward others? Is there a commonality
  in the people toward whom you do not have the
  same mind? For example, do you find that you
  do not have the same mind toward those who
  have a different educational background? Or
  social background? Toward whom do you have a
  haughty mind?*

» *Where have you fought for your preferences
  over others' desires? Where have you caused
  disunity because of pride? Is there a particular
  person that comes to mind? How can you live in
  harmony with that person this week?*

» *Write out a prayer of confession and ask the
  Lord to graciously help you "never be wise in
  your own sight" (Romans 12:16).*

4

Do Not Judge but Build up One Another

"Therefore let us not pass judgment on one another any longer, but rather decide never to put a stumbling block or hindrance in the way of a brother."

"So then let us pursue what makes for peace and for mutual upbuilding."

Romans 14:13; Romans 14:19

EXPLANATION

These two commands were written in the context (Romans 14) of judging others and causing others to stumble. Some people in the church at Rome were judging others because of what they ate. Paul was concerned about unity within the body of Christ. The apostle wrote, "So then each of us will give account of himself to God" (v. 12). One must be careful in thinking someone else is unspiritual or thinking what someone else does is unspiritual.

Realize that fostering harmony within the body of Christ

is Paul's primary interest in this passage. There should not be factions and judging but rather harmony and edification. The opposite of judging and tearing down is building up. The "one another" command in Romans 14:19 focuses on having peace within the body of Christ by the building up of one another.

Because of one's relationship with Jesus Christ, there is to be a peace at a horizontal level among fellow believers (this will be further explained in "Be at Peace with One Another"). There should not be factions. If there are cracks between the bricks, the building will not be strong. Bricks joined together in a building are dependent upon one another for strength and support. In the same way, believers need one another and should thus seek to build one another up. Each person should be building the other person up in his or her faith. The interests of the church should take a priority over the interests of self. Focusing on building up specific individuals will contribute to the building up of the church.

There is a stark contrast between verse 19 and verse 20 in Romans 14. Verse 19 speaks of building up while verse 20 speaks of tearing down. If believers are not pursuing things that make peace and things that build up, we are necessarily tearing down. There is no neutral position. One may not be intentionally tearing down, but such a person is doing just that by not building up.

Scripture commands that believers *pursue* the building up of one another. This does not suggest a lazy, apathetic approach to one's relationships with others. Rather, Scripture calls for a purposeful, deliberate, and urgent action among believers to build one another up.

ILLUSTRATION

In today's world, we often judge someone's spirituality by what we see externally. If people dress a certain way or do not do things according to our list of what a real "spiritual person" looks like, we judge them. If you were to write out what a spiritual person is, you would likely write a lot of things that would be measured by externals. You would have a list that looks like "They do this" and "They don't do this." This is an example of how we judge one another. Judging one another in this manner causes divisions and tears down others. Believers must take care that they do not hinder the exercise of their brothers' or sisters' faith.

APPLICATION

» *How have you judged others and torn them down? How does Matthew 7:1-5 apply to you?*

Judge not, that you be not judged. For with the judgment you pronounce you will be judged, and with the measure you use it will be measured to you. Why do you see the speck that is in your brother's eye, but do not notice the log that is in your own eye? Or how can you say to your brother, 'Let me take the speck out of your eye,' when there is the log in your own eye? You hypocrite, first take the log out of your own eye, and then you will see clearly to take the speck out of your brother's eye.
(Matthew 7:1-5)

» *Confess and repent of these. Determine how you can put away judging and tearing down, and put on building up.*

» *List several specific ways that you are currently "building up" one another. Who are the recipients of your action?*

» *1.*

» *2.*

» *3.*

» *Perhaps you are aware of a few "cracks" in the building. Who can be the recipient of your building up this week? How will you build up that person? What are the specific needs of this person? List them here. Be concrete and specific.*

» *1.*

» *2.*

» *3.*

» *For married couples, examine each other's strengths and weaknesses. How do you complement each other? How are you taking advantage of one another's strengths? How are you trying to build each other up in his or her respective weaknesses?*

	Husband	Wife
Strengths		
Weaknesses		
Plans for building up		

5

Welcome One Another

---

*"Therefore welcome one another as Christ has
welcomed you, for the glory of God."*

Romans 15:7

EXPLANATION

A s with the previous "one another" command, this command is also written in the context of judging others.
We see from Romans 14:1 that welcoming one another should
not be associated with judging one another. Because of their
unjustifiable judging, Christians in Rome were not welcoming one another, particularly when it came to Gentile believers. For the most part today, we do not have to deal with this
Jewish/Gentile distinction, but the principle remains the
same. We should welcome other believers without reserva-
tion.

To welcome or accept means more than "'tolerate' or 'give
official recognition to.'"[5] Believers can certainly "welcome"
one another as a formality or as a mere visible, outward act,
but this is not what Scripture calls for. Believers are to wel-

come one another in a genuine, heartfelt manner, "just as Christ also accepted us" (v. 7). This is also evident in Romans 14:3 where it is clear that one believer should accept another believer simply because of the fact that Jesus Christ has accepted both.

ILLUSTRATION

This welcoming one another is not delegated to a two-minute conversation at the worship service on Sunday. There is nothing wrong with greeting people around you with a handshake and saying, "Welcome." However, you have only a few moments to shake hands and briefly say, "Welcome, welcome, welcome." Instead, what if you use that time set aside in a service to seek out someone you do not know and just stop to ask a few questions to get to know him or her? Just say, "Hey, I want to get to know you. Let's talk after service." Get his or her name and jot down a few things about that person when you go back to your seat.

This "one another" command means not showing partiality, but receiving others, caring for them in Christ, and accepting them as Christ accepts us. So look past things like color, nationality, and anything that hinders us from welcoming others. We are to receive people and treat them like we would treat Jesus if he came into the room.

One should not just accept the ones who are more attractive or more acceptable in a worldly sense, but accept other believers without distinction. James 2, deals with this very issue:

> My brothers, show no partiality as you hold the faith in our Lord Jesus Christ, the Lord of glory. For if a man wearing a gold ring and fine clothing comes into your assembly, and a poor man in shabby clothing also comes in, and if you pay attention to the one

who wears the fine clothing and say, "You sit here in a good place," while you say to the poor man, "You stand over there," or, "Sit down at my feet," have you not then made distinctions among yourselves and become judges with evil thoughts?...But if you show partiality, you are committing sin and are convicted by the law as transgressors...For judgment is without mercy to one who has shown no mercy. Mercy triumphs over judgment.

(See the whole passage in James 2:1–13.)

APPLICATION

» *Does your welcoming one another come down to only a friendly handshake on Sunday morning? Look around you and note those believers who may appear to be left out. Who in your midst is feeling rejected by others? List them here. What can you do to make them accepted? Are you accepting them as Jesus accepted you? Are you doing this for God's glory? Seek to welcome these fellow believers this week.*

» *1.*

» *2.*

» *3.*

» *Are you accepting only those who are more "lovable"? What type of people are you less prone to accept and why? What is causing you to not accept one another? Is your reason justifiable by Scripture?*

» *How does your pride tend to make you look down on others or make it more difficult to welcome others? Confess your sins and repent of them; then seek to replace your pride with humility.*

6

Instruct One Another

---

*"I myself am satisfied about you, my brothers, that
you yourselves are full of goodness, filled with all
knowledge and able to instruct one another."*

Romans 15:14

EXPLANATION

Romans 15:14 should be understood in the context of what
Paul is addressing. As discussed previously, Paul states
that one should be careful about judging other believers and
then makes the point that a qualification for instructing is
that one is "full of goodness, filled with all knowledge." The
person instructing is one who seeks holiness of life and is
kind and generous like Christ—and has the right character
and the right understanding of Scripture. If the right character were not present, such a person would be criticized as
being a hypocrite. Ezra is a great example of a person who
studied the Word, practiced it, and then taught it (Ezra 7:10).
If people are wrong in their thinking, they are going to be
wrong in their living. Those who instruct one another should

want to help others think rightly so they may live rightly.

Keep in mind that one's desire to instruct another believer should be motivated by love for God and for the other person. If the one instructing does not truly want the other person to know Christ more intimately and to grow in faith, his motive may be questioned and his instruction suspect. One must be careful not to correct differences in preferences but only what is truly wrong or sinful.

ILLUSTRATION

Just being with people can bring some comfort and help but that is not all we are commanded to do. We must be asking questions and listening to what people are thinking and saying "out of the heart..." (Matthew 12:34). We must realize that people won't want what's right or do what's right if they don't think/believe what's right. This is where teaching—whether informally or formally—is particularly important. Pray for wisdom with regard to how much to say and when to say it.

APPLICATION

» *For most people, opportunities to instruct others are informal rather than formal. Most of our conversations are during informal times, not in classroom settings. Think of ways you can teach others during these times.*

» *Think of some recent missed opportunities to instruct others. Think of ways you can follow up.*

» *Consider whether the goal of your instruction aligns with Paul's goal expressed in the words of Colossians 1:28-29: "Him we proclaim, warning everyone and teaching everyone with all wisdom, that we may present everyone mature in Christ. For this I toil, struggling with all his energy that he powerfully works within me."*

7

Do Not Sue One Another

*"To have lawsuits at all with one another is already
a defeat for you. Why not rather suffer wrong? Why
not rather be defrauded?"*

1 Corinthians 6:7

EXPLANATION

"Lawsuits contribute to the disintegration of a society
and cause individualism to reign supreme. When this
happens, loving concern for one's neighbor is extinguished
in an atmosphere of rank egoism."[6] This is a powerful statement by Simon J. Kistemaker, but it rings true as this is what
Paul writes to the Corinthian church in 1 Corinthians 6:1-8.
Basically, Paul is stating that a believer should not take another believer to court.

Paul's word order in the Greek manuscript is interesting
here. "Already" is emphatic, coming first in the sentence. Paul
is saying that before one even goes to court against another
believer, he has *already* lost. Lost what? Paul is not talking

about losing the specific legal issue about which one goes to court, but rather one has lost his testimony of Jesus Christ before the unbelieving world. By going to a pagan court of law to settle an issue with another believer, the Christian has shown defeat. He or she has shown the unbelieving world that Christian love is not fervent and forgiving, and that it does not cover a multitude of sins (1 Peter 4:8). He or she has shown that believers are no different than unbelievers. He or she has shown that being a Christian does not mean one can forgive others and has shown that Christ's teaching about unity and love is not enough to overcome the desire to seek one's personal rights. Defeat occurs before the trial even happens. The world screams about individual rights and proving oneself right, but this is not what Scripture teaches should be so of believers.

If you are facing an issue with one who professes to be a believer but who appears to be an unbeliever (has no fruit, lives for self, does not belong to a church, etc.), you should consult with church leaders about this command. It would be best to try to implement other principles of Scripture such as, "If possible, so far as it depends on you, live peaceably with all" (Romans 12:18).

This does not mean that this person who has caused the issue should be free to run rampant in his sin. Sometimes, the legal system can hinder his actions by declaring a judgment against him. In this type of situation, you should prayerfully seek godly counsel from church leadership before proceeding, as there may be many complicating factors involved in how you should handle it in a God-honoring way. Every situation is unique, so it is important for you to seek godly advice.

ILLUSTRATION

Let's unpack this a little bit. Let's say your car was rear-ended. In this case, it is not you taking someone else to court, but your insurance company taking that person's insurance company to court. That is not the same thing as taking a fellow believer to court. Rather, this text is speaking of a brother and sister going downtown to the court to sue another believer.

In another example, a contractor said he would do a job and bailed out, taking all your money. Do you take that person who professes to be a Christian to court? You should definitely get the church leadership involved in a situation like this. If there is a personal wrong, consult with your church leaders for their wisdom, counsel, and prayers. There may be a lot of variables that need to be weighed. Get your church leadership involved to make a God-honoring decision.

APPLICATION

» *Have you ever experienced an unfulfilled or broken legal contract with another believer? How did you handle it then? How would you handle it now?*

» *Perhaps you are currently in the middle of litigation with a professing believer. If so, how does this "one another" command apply to you?*

» *If you have been wronged by another professing believer, pray about the situation and seek counsel from your pastor for ways to settle this matter without turning to the unbelieving court system.*

8

Care for One Another

"...that there may be no division in the body, but that the members may have the same care for one another."

1 Corinthians 12:25

EXPLANATION

It is clear from the "one another" commands and the general teaching of Scripture that unity is important in the body of Christ. Most believers would state that they want unity, but most would be at a loss as to how to attain that unity. Here in 1 Corinthians 12:25, Paul provides one way to achieve that unity—that is, not to have division—and that is by caring for one another.

The context of this passage is important in gaining a proper understanding of this command. Chapter 12 of 1 Corinthians teaches about spiritual matters and the variety of gifts that may be present in a local church. Even with the variety, there should be unity. Paul uses an illustration of the human body to show the unity that needs to exist in the body of Jesus Christ. Each part of the physical body is important for the proper function of other parts. Each part affects the other parts. We cannot say that one part is not important. If one part rejoices, other parts should rejoice; if one part suffers, all the parts should suffer along with it. It is in this context that Paul says, "Have the same care for one another" (v. 25). In other words, a believer must care for others equally and without discrimination, understanding that each part of the body is important. The less honorable parts are equally deserving of care as the more honorable parts. The weaker parts should be cared for as much as the stronger parts. Those who are less visible should receive care as much as those who are more visible.

ILLUSTRATION

Caring for one another is not just having an affectionate *feeling* toward another believer. Caring is not merely an emotional feeling, just as love is not merely a feeling. Both care and love are actions. One's care of another must be displayed by specific actions. Practically speaking, do regular members of the congregation get less care and attention than the lead pastor of the congregation? For example, if you heard that a pastor's refrigerator had broken down, would you consider helping with that? However, if the refrigerator of that quiet church member who sits in the corner broke down, would you react the same way? Do you give Christmas presents to the pastor but not to the deacons? It takes effort and diligence to make sure you care for others without discrimination. Certain groups should not get special treatment; certain groups should not get worse treatment either. With each person seeking to care for others, there will be a visible difference in the unity of the body of Christ.

APPLICATION

» *Look through your church directory and make a note of specific individuals for whom you have neglected to care. Or maybe you have neglected to care for your roommate, spouse, children, parents, small-group member or some other person. Do you notice a pattern in whom you care for and whom you do not care for? If so, confess and repent of your lack of care for others as emphasized in the "one another" passages of Scripture. Note specific acts you can do for those whom you have neglected to show care. Be specific and write down a time and place to act with care. There is always some way you can practically care for others.*

» *1.*

» *2.*

» *3.*

9

Do Not Provoke and Do Not Envy One Another

---

*"Let us not become conceited, provoking one
another, envying one another."*

Galatians 5:26

EXPLANATION

This could be two separate "one another" commands, but we will look at them together. Galatians 5:25-26 say, "If we live by the Spirit, let us also keep in step with the Spirit. Let us not become conceited, provoking one another, envying one another."

Provoking is a temptation of the strong in the faith as they relate to the weak in the faith. This was a big issue going on for the Galatians. Provoking is a temptation to the strong in the faith to flaunt their liberty with the weak in the faith. The provoking spirit says, "You are struggling with that? Not me." Rather than using their liberty to serve one another, the strong in the faith use it for an occasion of the flesh, to flaunt it, provoking those who are weak in the faith. Do not use your liberty for an occasion of the flesh.

Envy happens to be what the weak may feel toward the strong. The envious spirit says, "I wish I didn't have trouble with my conscience so I could live the way you live." The weak, typically the young in the faith with a bound-up conscience adhere to many laws which they themselves have added. Envying is equally as sinful as provoking.

ILLUSTRATION

The law versus grace, or the law versus gospel movement, comes into play here. Those on the side of the law, who go too far, get all tied up with the "dos and don'ts," sometimes going way beyond what Scripture says. They create their own standard of holiness or rules to follow according to their own thinking. On the "gospel only" side, you find those who do all kinds of stuff in their liberty with no concern for others. Those flaunting the drinking of alcohol in front of others who are opposed to the consumption of alcohol is an example of this. Stay away from both envy and provocation, for freedom should take you toward holiness instead of calamity.

APPLICATION

» *If you have been a believer for some time and have grown in your faith, are you flaunting your liberty in Christ to those around you? Do you talk about all the stuff you do, such as praying or abstaining from sinful television, thus provoking new believers or those who are weak in faith?*

»   *Though you may not realize you are doing this,
    you are boasting. When you do this, you are
    causing the weak in the faith to struggle and
    might be provoking them to anger.*

»   *Whom do you find yourself provoking and why?
    Confess and repent of your sins.*

»   1.

»   2.

»   3.

»   *If you are new in the faith, your awakened
    conscience may have added all kinds of laws,
    perhaps stated like "You must do this, and you
    must not do that." Maybe you find yourself
    envying those who are more mature in the faith
    who seem not to be bothered by certain things.
    Your whole attitude really needs to be one of
    humility—walking and keeping in step with the
    Spirit.*

»   *Whom do you find yourself envying and why?
    What is it that you envy about such people?
    Confess your sin and repent of it.*

»   1.

»   2.

»   3.

10

Bear One Another's Burdens

*"Bear one another's burdens, and so fulfill
the law of Christ."*

Galatians 6:2

EXPLANATION

This passage deals with helping a fellow believer who is going through a difficult trial. It is the responsibility of fellow believers to assist and help carry that burden. We can picture someone physically getting underneath someone else's burden to help shoulder it, like two oxen under a yoke. You get up underneath and help shoulder it because the person would otherwise be crushed by carrying the weight of the burden alone. A believer in Jesus Christ should not have to endure difficult trials by himself. It is the responsibility of fellow believers to help other Christians carry whatever heavy loads they are presently enduring. By obeying this "one another" command to bear one another's burdens, believers create a beautiful picture of Christian unity and love.

Christians often say, "I'll pray for you" when they hear

of others' burdens but bearing one another's burdens goes beyond saying a prayer, although it certainly does include prayers. Prayers should go hand in hand with action (1 John 3:18). The goal is to come alongside and shoulder the weight together with the other person. One thing to keep in mind is that this "one another" command does not mean you need to take on the *entire* burden of the other person. Verse 5 says, "For each one will bear his own load." For example, if someone is depressed and her apartment is a mess, you should not clean her entire apartment by yourself but rather *help* her clean her own apartment. It should not be "I'll do it for you" but rather, "I'll help you. We will get this done *together*."

As Paul writes, bearing one another's burdens "fulfills the law of Christ." By bearing one another's burdens, a believer is fulfilling the greatest commandments given by God to people—to love God and love one's neighbors (Matthew 22:36 ff.). This physical act of assisting a brother in need portrays the intent of God's desire for all believers.

ILLUSTRATION

Some years ago, there was an international student who did not have much money as his student visa did not allow him to take on a job. He was embarrassed about his financial situation and would not tell anyone. One day, it became obvious he was physically sick and unable to shake off a chronic cough. A student said to him, "You need to see a doctor. As a matter of fact, go to the clinic on campus." The international student just nodded. The other student said, "I want you to go to the clinic. Make sure you go. I really care for you and am going to pray for you that you feel better." The professor noticed the interaction and asked the international student, "Do you have enough money to pay to go to the clinic?" His answer was no. So the entire class took a collection and gave him the money, enough to cover the appointment and prescription if needed. This is the perfect picture of bearing one another's burdens. It is not just praying for the person but also actually getting under the yoke and helping that person. If you cannot meet the need yourself, figure out a way to meet it. We are really fast to say, "I'll pray for you." While bearing one another's burdens includes prayer, it just does not end there.

APPLICATION

» *Consider carefully and list the names of those who are going through difficult trials in their lives. Explain in detail how you will help bear each person's burden in the days and weeks to come.*

» 1.

» 2.

» 3.

» *Reflect upon how God has brought others into your life to help you bear your burdens. Give thanks to God and perhaps write a note of thanks and encouragement to those individuals.*

» 1.

» 2.

» 3.

11

Speak Truthfully to One Another

"Therefore, having put away falsehood, let each one of you speak the truth with his neighbor, for we are members one of another."

"Addressing one another in psalms and hymns and spiritual songs, singing and making melody to the Lord with your heart."

Ephesians 4:25; Ephesians 5:19

EXPLANATION

After providing three chapters of doctrinal teaching about Christ and the church, Paul enters into a discussion of very practical matters related to the church. Ephesians 4:25's "one another" command is written in the context of having unity in the body of Christ. There is a strong emphasis for believers to seek to be one in Christ.

Truth is such a foundational aspect of a trusting relationship. Without truthfulness, a biblical relationship cannot occur. How can there be a loving relationship if that relationship is based on falsehood and lies? Repeated lies destroy the trust in a relationship and the basis of a good relationship is damaged. Lying should not characterize a believer; rather, the speaking of truth should characterize a believer.

Not only must one speak the truth, but one must speak the truth *in love*. Ephesians 4:15 reads, "Rather, speaking the truth in love." Truth not spoken in love can be quite harmful. For example, if you see a woman wearing a beautiful black dress, you may say, "Your outfit is beautiful today. You should wear this more often." These are true statements. However, if these statements were made at a funeral and the woman had just lost her husband, it would be inappropriate. Even though these were true statements, they had not been spoken with love for the benefit of the hearer. Truth must be spoken at the appropriate time, under the appropriate circumstances, and in the appropriate manner, or it is not spoken in love. As James 3 teaches, the tongue is a powerful thing, and one must be careful how it is used.

ILLUSTRATION

There are people at church who face ongoing struggles but when they are asked how they are doing, they just say, "Fine." Sometimes this is not the truth. Instead of saying, "I'm fine" perhaps a better response would be, "I'm doing okay, thanks, but it's hard." Others would really appreciate such true statements. This allows us to respond with words such as "Is there anything in particular I can pray for? Is there anything specific I can do to help or encourage you?" You can then set up a time to meet up and discuss matters in more depth. Not every response to "How are you doing?" on a Sunday morning needs to turn into a thirty-minute discussion, but a truthful response can lead to profitable opportunities for ministry.

Here is another example of not speaking the truth. Sometimes people say they love a certain kind of food, when in reality they really hate it. There was a young man who was dating a girl and she made him a particular casserole. He raved about the casserole in front of her and others when she was around. But when she was not around, he would say how much he hated tuna casserole. We can understand he didn't want to offend her, but this continued for years, even into their marriage, and only later did she find out that he hated tuna casserole. Imagine the disappointment and embarrassment! How much better would it have been for him to kindly let her know early on that he did not care for tuna casserole! She said, "You mean for the past couple of years you've been lying?" Her mind was filling with other thoughts like "What else? What else have you said that you love that you hate? What else have you lied about?" Even though his intention was good, not speaking the truth ultimately turned into something far more harmful. Speak the truth in love. Be honest, be kind, be gracious.

APPLICATION

» *Do you recall a recent conversation when you did not speak the truth? If so, confess it now and repent of your sin. Contact the person who heard you so that you can confess your sin and seek that person's forgiveness.*

» *Do you recall a recent conversation when the truth was not spoken in love? What did you do? What should you have done?*

» *When are you most prone to not speak the truth? What are the circumstances surrounding those times? Do you see a particular pattern in your speech that needs correcting?*

» *An excellent resource for you to use is John Crotts' book "Graciousness: Tempering Truth with Love" (Grand Rapids, MI: Reformation Heritage Books, 2018).*

12

Be Kind to One Another

"Be kind to one another, tenderhearted, forgiving one
another, as God in Christ forgave you."

Ephesians 4:32

EXPLANATION

An important principle of Scripture (and of biblical counseling) is this "put off" and "put on" model. Sinful habits
must be replaced with new godly habits. If one must put on
the qualities mentioned in verse 32 (being kind to one another), one must of necessity put off the qualities of verse
31 (bitterness, wrath, anger, clamor, slander, and all malice).

What is this kindness? It is very interesting to note that
the same Greek root word for kind used in Ephesians 4:32 is
also used in Romans 2:4 to describe God's attitude toward
believers before their salvation. Romans 2:4 asks, "Or do you
presume on the riches of his kindness and forbearance and
patience, not knowing that God's kindness is meant to lead
you to repentance?" How amazing! While the Bible often
presents God's certain and coming wrath as a reason to re-

pent, here Paul highlights God's kindness as the motivation to turn to him. God's tenderheartedness and his forgiveness are what draw sinners to Jesus Christ. Believers are called to show the same kindness that they received at salvation to their fellow believers.

ILLUSTRATION

This principle is true even in the most basic things, such as talking to one another. Proverbs 15:1 states that "A soft answer turns away wrath, but a harsh word stirs up anger." Imagine someone coming up to you fuming with anger and using harsh words. How would you respond? If, on the other hand, a person came to you with much gentleness and sweetness of speech, you would be much more receptive. This is how believers are to treat one another. Kindness should be a hallmark of a believer's life.

APPLICATION

» *The chart following summarizes the put off / put on teaching of Ephesians 4:22–32. Think of a recent incident where you were not kind to a fellow believer, and jot down in the left column how you did not put off and put on. What will be your first step in being kind to one another?*

Ephesians 4	Put Off	Put On
vv. 22-24	The old self, which belongs to your former manner of life and is corrupt through deceitful desires	The new self, created after the likeness of God in true righteousness and holiness.
v. 25	Put away falsehood.	Speak the truth
v. 28	No longer steal	Labor doing honest work with [your] own hands
v. 29	Let no corrupting word come out of your mouths	But only such as is good for building up, as fits the occasion, that it may give grace to those who hear.
vv. 31-32	Let all bitterness and wrath and anger and clamor and slander be put away from you, along with all malice.	Be tenderhearted, forgiving one another, as God in Christ forgave you.

13

Forgive One Another

"Be kind to one another, tenderhearted, forgiving one another, as God in Christ forgave you."

"bearing with one another and, if one has a complaint against another, forgiving each other; as the Lord has forgiven you, so you also must forgive."

Ephesians 4:32; Colossians 3:13

EXPLANATION

"I'm really sorry about that." "Please accept my apologies." These empty statements have replaced "Please forgive me," even by many Christians. Many believers today sin because they do not truly forgive one another. The lack of forgiveness may occur because they refuse to grant forgiveness or simply because they lack understanding of biblical forgiveness.

In today's feeling-oriented society, people have confused granting forgiveness with overlooking sin, excusing sin, or accepting apologies. However, Scripture is very clear about exactly what forgiveness is. Simply stated, forgiveness is a matter of obedience. Luke 17:1–10 explains this clearly. When Jesus spoke about repeated forgiveness, the disciples thought they needed more faith to be able to forgive repeatedly. They said, "Increase our faith!" (v. 5). Jesus, however, wanted to teach the disciples that the issue was not about the lack of faith, but rather about the lack of obedience. Jesus pointedly illustrated this important truth by showing how a servant does what he does simply because of who the master is and because of who he is in relation to the master. Likewise, Christians should forgive one another simply because of who their Master is—the Lord Jesus Christ. Forgiveness is not about feelings or even about the lack of faith; forgiveness is simply a matter of obedience.

Basically, Scripture is clear that there is both a *method* and a *manner* in which to forgive (Matthew 18:15–35; Luke 17:1–4). The method is as follows: If someone sins against you, go and talk to him. If he confesses and repents, it is your responsibility to then forgive. If he listens to you and responds biblically, then the issue is done. If not, you then bring someone else with you.

Jesus forgives lovingly, quickly, repeatedly, and lavishly. When we come to God and ask for forgiveness, God does it very quickly and consistently. That is the same manner in which we should forgive.

ILLUSTRATION

Another important aspect of believers forgiving one another is that we should understand that forgiveness involves both a heart attitude of love and a willingness to forgive, as well as a transaction upon confession. One must seek forgiveness and one must grant forgiveness (Luke 17:3). Many Christian relationships are unresolved because this transaction is not occurring. People often just say, "I'm so sorry. Please accept my apologies." The popular worldly response is, "Well, that's okay," or, "Okay, apology accepted." What do these statements accomplish? Nothing, really. However, when people seek and grant forgiveness in terms that the Bible describes, a wonderful transaction occurs. As Jay Adams points out, in granting forgiveness a promise is made that involves the following three statements:

* I will not bring the matter up to you.

* I will not bring the matter up to another.

* I will not bring the matter up to myself.[7]

The following statement is unbiblical: "Forgive and forget." When Christians forgive one another, they are not promising that they will never remember what occurred. Rather, they are promising that they will not bring up the forgiven charge again in the future, to themselves or anyone else.

APPLICATION

» *List names of people from whom you need to seek forgiveness. Write out in detail exactly what you will say as you confess and seek forgiveness from that person (see Luke 15:18–19). Also confess and repent of your sins to God.*

» *Are there people who have asked for your forgiveness whom you have not granted forgiveness? If so, take appropriate steps to forgive them in a biblical manner.*

» *This command for believers to forgive one another is an important issue to understand in helping people resolve problems in their relationships. An excellent resource is "Unpacking Forgiveness: Biblical Answers for Complex Questions and Deep Wounds" by Chris Brauns (Crossway 2008).*

14

Be in Submission to One Another

*"Submitting to one another out of
reverence for Christ."*

Ephesians 5:21

EXPLANATION

Submission is an "old military figure to line up under (Colossians 3:18)."[8] A soldier does not choose which higher
ranking officer he should submit to and which officer he
should not submit to. A private always submits to the general. This is what needs to happen in the relationships of believers with one another. This passage is not talking about
mutual submission, and neither does the Bible teach mutual
submission. God has sovereignly and specifically placed a
certain authority structure around each individual.

The submission mentioned in verse 21 does not contradict
passages that follow; rather, it complements them. Wives are
to be subject to their own husbands (v. 24), children are to
obey and honor their parents (6:1-2), and slaves are to obey
their masters (vv. 5-8). Each of the preceding points is an

example of believers being subject to one another.

The following passages expand upon the "one another" submission of Ephesians 5:21, "submitting to one another out of reverence for Christ."

* *Submission to Christ:* "But I want you to understand that the head of every man is Christ..." (1 Corinthians 11:3a)
* *Submission to Husbands:* "Wives, submit to your own husbands, as to the Lord." (Ephesians 5:22)
* *Submission to Parents:* "Children, obey your parents in the Lord, for this is right." (Ephesians 6:1)
* *Submission to Masters/Employers:*[9] "Bondservants, obey your earthly masters with fear and trembling, with a sincere heart, as you would Christ." (Ephesians 6:5)
* *Submission to Spiritual Leaders:* "Obey your leaders and submit to them, for they are keeping watch over your souls, as those who will have to give an account. Let them do this with joy and not with groaning, for that would be of no advantage to you." (Hebrews 13:17)
* *Submission to Government:* "Let every person be subject to the governing authorities. For there is no authority except from God, and those that exist have been instituted by God." (Romans 13:1)

ILLUSTRATION

Be careful of the example of slaves and masters in Ephesians 6. This is often pushed too much into the workplace. If you are an employee, you are not a slave and your boss is not your master. Today's workplace is not equivalent to what was going on at the time of Roman slavery. Today, you can quit and find another job. There are certain principles here, however, that you can observe and use. When you work, do not work just to please your master but to please God, "...not by the way of eye-service, as people-pleasers, but as bondservants of Christ, doing the will of God from the heart..." (v. 6).

Do not say you think you have to stay at a certain place of employment simply because God has led you there. Do not put God's name on everything that you yourself are doing, saying, and choosing. You chose to work there and that is fine. You can use that for the glory of God. If you say, "I think I can work in a different job with better hours as that would fit better with my schedule," you have the freedom to do that. Sometimes we unthinkingly claim God has guided us in the desires and urges that come from our hearts. It's best just to leave God with his commands, principles, and the Scriptures, and then to make the best-informed decisions possible.

Application

» *How is submission going in your life? Are you in submission to the appropriate authorities? Are you having trouble with people who are in authority over your life?*

» *What about your parents, if you are still under their authority and not financially independent from them?*

» *Are you in submission to church leadership, to God and his Word, and to the government?*

» *Is there someone from whom you need to ask forgiveness because you are rebellious in a realm such as these?*

15

Bear with One Another

"Bearing with one another and, if one has a complaint against another, forgiving each other; as the Lord has forgiven you, so you also must forgive."

Colossians 3:13

EXPLANATION

Colossians 3:13 must be read in context with the preceding verse, "Put on then, as God's chosen ones, holy and beloved, compassionate hearts, kindness, humility, meekness, and patience." This is a reference to how we are to endure and put up with one another when there is not an obvious sin—and this means putting up with one another's imperfections, putting up with the strange values of one another, and putting up with one another's idiosyncrasies and habits. There are things that people do that can rub you the wrong way, but God's Word says we are to bear with others—even the ones we find unlikeable. Be it a roommate, a sibling, a spouse, or other church members, we are to bear with one another.

Why is it that people get annoyed with other people?

The person being annoying may not, in fact, be at the root of this annoyance. Sometimes, the root of the problem may actually be the one who gets annoyed. When someone easily gets annoyed with others, it is pride rearing its ugly head. The person with the feeling of annoyance is basically saying that he himself is less annoying than the other person. He thinks that he himself has no annoying qualities and that the fault lies entirely with the other person. This is an arrogant thought! In a way, the person feeling annoyed is saying he is better than the other person. It is impossible to see others correctly when there is a log in one's own eye. Matthew 7:1-5 states that you are to

> Judge not, that you be not judged. For with the judgment you pronounce you will be judged, and with the measure you use it will be measured to you. Why do you see the speck that is in your brother's eye, but do not notice the log that is in your own eye? Or how can you say to your brother, "Let me take the speck out of your eye," when there is the log in your own eye? You hypocrite, first take the log out of your own eye, and then you will see clearly to take the speck out of your brother's eye.

You need to carefully examine your own heart before allowing yourself to get annoyed with others. Christians should actively seek to bear with one another. It is vital that believers repent of any pride in their hearts and bear with one another, remembering that others have to bear with them as well!

ILLUSTRATION

This "putting up with one another" is like oil in the engine because it makes all the parts work together smoothly. Without such lubrication, regular daily rubs begin to irritate, and before long, they become unbearable. Keep in mind that as you put up with others, they have to put up with you as well.

If there are unpleasant traits that are preventing a person from making disciples or winning the lost, this matter needs to be addressed, especially if a believer is characterized by strange or weird behavior that so that it is unpleasant and hard for others to be around them. Believers are called to share the gospel and make disciples. It's not right just to say, "That's just the way I am," and refuse to change. With the enabling of the Holy Spirit, a Christian is able to change. It may mean that some help is needed, especially if he is unaware of what he is doing (or if he knows but does not care). If this is you, you need to be aware and you need to care because you cannot invest in the lives of others if no one wants to be around you.

APPLICATION

» *How have you displayed impatience to a fellow believer?*

» *Under what circumstances or situations do you find it most difficult to "bear with one another"? List three of them below and suggest how this chapter might help you to act more consistently as a "one another" Christian.*

» *1.*

» *2.*

» *3.*

» *Read Matthew 7:1-5 and examine your own life. How are you making it difficult for people to*

*deal with you? Are you causing unnecessary
"patient forbearance" in another believer's life?
Perhaps ask some close friends—people who will
speak the truth to you in love—for their input.
List at least three things about yourself that you
can change.*

» 1.

» 2.

» 3.

» *Perhaps in the workplace unbelievers are talking
about believers and how weird they are (and not
because of their faith but because of their traits).
If so, believers there need to acknowledge that,
confess it, and make some changes. You might
have to point out to other believers how they
come across in conversations—so maybe you
could give them a hand signal or find a way to
make them aware of their irritating trait. Try to
alert the believer so his or her actions don't turn
others away.*

16

Teach and Admonish One Another

*"Let the word of Christ dwell in you richly, teaching
and admonishing one another in all wisdom,
singing psalms and hymns and spiritual songs, with
thankfulness in your hearts to God."*

Colossians 3:16

EXPLANATION

The Greek word for admonish, *noutheteo*, is difficult to translate with a precise English meaning. Many scholars have translated it, depending on its context, as *admonish*, *warn*, *exhort*, *counsel*, *instruct*, and *teach*. Jay Adams says that this word can be understood by examining it "as a concept and as a practice."[10] He also notes that the word is frequently used in conjunction with teaching, with problem solving, and with the intent of correction for the benefit of the counselee.[11] The term "nouthetic" counseling comes from this word (cf. Colossians 1:28-29).

Believers are filled with the Spirit (controlled by the Spirit) when they are filled with God's Word (controlled by God's

Word). How is this possible? When you examine the text of Ephesians 5:15-20 and Colossians 3:16-17, you will see an obvious parallel. The chart following shows this clearly.

Ephesians 4	Ephesians 5	Colossians 3
Wisdom	15 Look carefully then how you walk, not as unwise as wise, 16 making the best use of the time, because the days are evil. 17 Therefore do not be foolish, but understand what the will of the Lord is.	16b With all wisdom
Dwelling	18 And do not get drunk with wine, for that is debauchery, but be filled with the Spirit,	16a Let the word of Christ dwell in you richly
Loosened tongue	19 addressing one another in psalms and hymns and spiritual songs, singing and making melody to the Lord with your heart,	16b teaching and admonishing one another in all wisdom, singing psalms and hymns and spiritual songs, with thankfulness in your hearts to God.
Thanksgiving	20 giving thanks always and for everything to God the Father in the name of our Lord Jesus Christ.	17 And whatever you do in word or deed, do everything in the name of the Lord Jesus, giving thanks to God the Father through him.

There is a remarkable parallel between the two passages. A wise person will understand God's will and be filled with the Spirit (Ephesians 5:18). The result of being filled with the Spirit will be a loosened tongue that sings praises and gives thanks to God (vv. 19-20). The result is similar in Colossians 3:16ff. A person with God's Word dwelling in his life (v. 16a), has a tongue loosened to teach, admonish, sing, and give thanks (vv. 16-17)! Thus, the result of being filled with the Spirit (Ephesians) and the result of having God's Word dwelling within (Colossians) is the same: a loosened tongue to teach, sing, and give thanks. In this way, being Spirit filled is being filled with God's Word.

As a result of being filled with God's Word, believers should teach one another with all humility. In a general sense, teaching is not only something done by the appointed elders and pastors, but it is done by everyone. Believers are to take every opportunity to teach one another the great truths of God whenever they can—and this may take place not only in formal Bible studies but also during times of singing. Making use of songs that are biblically oriented and faithful to the text of Scripture may and should be used in teaching one another. Christians can share playlists and albums with spiritual songs to encourage and teach spiritual truths. Music is a powerful tool for teaching truth, provided, of course, the lyrics are biblical in content.

ILLUSTRATION

Making use of psalms, hymns, and music is an aspect of ministering to one another that can be very effective. Hymn authors and composers have, for generations, taught and admonished people by means of music. Many writers of hymns memorized large portions of Scripture—so when you sing them, you will be able to identify where certain stanzas come from in Scripture. The writers had Scripture dwelling richly in their minds as they wrote their compositions.

In some churches today, the songs used in worship are anemic if they are evaluated in light of robust biblical content. The tunes and beat are often catchy, but there is a lack of good theology because the lyrics are simply not Word-oriented. In fact, some content is so much in error that, if you know your Bible, you find yourself thinking, "Wow, that was wrong!" And how sad it is that you cannot even sing some of the songs with a good conscience, as you would be singing error—even if everyone likes the tune.

If you are involved in music ministry, be really careful to ensure that both the content and composition of songs you use show faithfulness to the Bible, are honoring to God, and will be helpful in light of ministering to others. Having the Word of Christ dwelling in you richly will help keep you from error.

APPLICATION

» *Even though you may not have a formal Bible education, do you desire to teach others what God is teaching you? List three people you can "teach" this week (even in informal or spontaneous conversation) as you talk about what God is doing in your life.*

» *1.*

» *2.*

» *3.*

» *Write down how you are (or are not) living a Spirit-filled life—that is, Spirit-controlled life— in God's Word.*

» *Consider sharing verses from a hymn or a praise song that is soundly biblical with someone who can benefit from what it teaches. List three people and outline what you would like to share with them.*

» 1.

» 2

» 3.

17

Increase and Abound in Love
for One Another

"And may the Lord make you increase and abound in love for one another and for all, as we do for you."

1 Thessalonians 3:12

EXPLANATION

The command to love one another is used over a dozen times in the New Testament. This is perhaps the one command that sums up all the other "one another" commands. In a sense, one can say that all the other "one another" commands are an expression of this one command to "love one another"—as mentioned in the chapter *Introduction: A Word About Relationships*. If one word could describe the Christian relationship, it should be "love." The text 1 Corinthians 13:4-8a is probably the "premier" wedding sermon passage—and for good reason! One cannot help but be humbled in reading, "Love is patient and kind; love does not envy or boast; it is not arrogant or rude. It does not insist on its own way; it is not irritable or resentful; it does not rejoice at wrongdoing, but rejoices with the truth. Love bears all things, believes all things, hopes all things, endures all things. Love never ends..." Note that all of these words describing love are verbs; they are words denoting action. In other words, these are all words of *motion,* not *emotion.* There is no direct link between love and feelings here. One should be careful to not mix unbiblical "feelings" with the term "love." God's type of love is primarily an act of obedience—a command that believers must obey.

In 1 Thessalonians, the term "increase and abound" carries a sense of something overflowing.[12] Believers should have so much love for one another that it even flows toward unbelievers. Love abounds to all people.

Like Jesus' love for us, our love for one another should be unconditional. If a believer's love is conditional, what good will it be? If love is conditional, one is only seeking to serve self. Matthew 5:43-48 shows an excellent picture of how love should not be conditional. It is easy to love those who can return the love. Even the most wretched unbeliever is capable of doing good to those who would return the favor. But, what about loving those who cannot return the love? Jesus speaks to this issue in Matthew 5:43-48:

> You have heard that it was said, 'You shall love your neighbor and hate your enemy.' But I say to you, Love your enemies and pray for those who persecute you, so that you may be sons of your Father who is in heaven. For he makes his sun rise on the evil and on the good, and sends rain on the just and on the unjust. For if you love those who love you, what reward do you have? Do not even the tax collectors do the same? And if you greet only your brothers, what more are you doing than others? Do not even the Gentiles do the same? You therefore must be perfect, as your heavenly Father is perfect.

Is it easy to love those who do not return the love? No. Does that mean Christians should not love them? Again, the answer is no. A believer can love another person, even an enemy, and pray for that person because God works in the life of a regenerate person (Philippians 2:13) and enables him or her to obey God's commands. Again, the ability to love one's neighbor *and* one's enemy should be a distinctive feature of a Christian's life.[13]

ILLUSTRATION

Many times a day, Tom told his newlywed wife he loved her. Yet, Joyce kept asking him, "Do you love me?" Tom could not figure out why she kept asking that question when he would say, "I love you" to her multiple times a day. Tom wondered whether it was perhaps because Joyce was from a broken home or had previously experienced difficulties and that she just needed plenty of affirmation. However, the reason Joyce kept repeating her question was that she felt Tom's profession of love was nothing more than words—and there was no action to back them up. In the same way, this "one another" command to love fellow believers is not just limited to words. Rather, the words must express themselves in concrete fashion! When you say you love someone and then show it, you will not be asked, "Do you love me?"

APPLICATION

» *How are you seeking to fulfill the commandment in John 13:34-35, "A new commandment I give to you, that you love one another: just as I have loved you, you also are to love one another. By this all people will know*

*that you are my disciples, if you have love for
one another"?*

» *List the three "one another" commands that are
most difficult for you to implement in your life.
Explain why this is the case and note how you
will seek to be obedient to them.*

» 1.

» 2.

» 3.

» *Make a list of three people you need to love. How
have you been neglecting to love them? Repent
of your lack of love for them and identify specific
acts of love you can show them. Remember, love
is an action—not just a feeling.*

» 1.

» 2.

» 3.

18

Comfort One Another

"Therefore encourage one another with these words."

1 Thessalonians 4:18

EXPLANATION

Jim Phillips in his commentary mentions some of the world's common sayings: "Don't worry, everything will turn out all right," "Well, give it time. Time will heal," and "Cheer up—it could be worse."[14] Do these words really convey any sense of hope or comfort? Even Christians have some of their own trite sayings—sayings like: "God is sovereign," "God knows," and "Look to Jesus." These words may be spoken in an effort to be helpful and "spiritual." But even these Christian phrases (as true as they are) can be a source of little comfort when spoken tritely. Where, then, do believers find this comfort?

We can see the answer in how the Thessalonians were comforted in 1 Thessalonians 4. The term for comfort used in v. 18 is the same Greek word that is often used for "encourage" in other places of Scripture (1 Thessalonians 5:11; Colossians 4:8). Here, in 1 Thessalonians 4:18, the context makes it clear that the meaning is "comfort."

Christians in Thessalonica thought Christ had already returned. To them, this meant God had not fulfilled his promise of a bodily resurrection for their loved ones in the grave. So Paul ufolded the truth of God's Word that Christ had not returned yet. In doing so, the Thessalonnains were encouraged with specific teaching that brought a true and eternal perspective to their concerns and their thinking.

True comfort comes not from limited human wisdom or a quicky dispensed phrase but rather from the ministry of the very words of God—that is, the Word carefully and compassionately unfolded within a sufferer's difficult, fearful, or sorrowful context. Romans 15:4 states, "For whatever was written in former days was written for our instruction, that through endurance and through the encouragement of the Scriptures we might have hope." There is comfort for those who mourn over their spiritual depravity and sins (Matthew 5:4). There is comfort in the promise of forgiveness (1 John 1:9). There is also comfort in the character and promises of God as stated in 1 Corinthians 10:13. In that passage, the very character of God—namely his faithfulness—gives comfort and hope.

So, believers need to use God's Word to bring comfort to one another, just as Paul did with the Thessalonian church in 1 Thessalonians 4:14-17.

And, immediately after a magnificent description of what will happen to those who died before the return of Jesus Christ, Paul says, "Therefore encourage one another with these words" (v. 18). Believers can lose focus and be in despair when they focus too much on the things of this world. There is always a need for an eternal perspective on life and not being so nearsighted as to forget God and the great promises he has made in his Word. We can bring real comfort and hope by encouraging one another with his words (Psalm 119:49,50; Psalm 19:7,8),

Illustration

Merely talking to a friend about one's difficulties or afflictions brings nothing more than a temporary *sense of* relief— if even that. It is better to encourage people in your conversation, reminding them that the Lord is returning and today is one day closer to that reality. Be watchfully waiting while praying like the apostle John is described in Revelation, saying, "Lord please come quickly" (see Revelation 22.20). The Puritan Richard Baxter, when he was told he was going to die, read everything about heaven and he concluded this: If we are not heavenly minded—thinking about heaven, Christ's return, etc.—we will not be of much earthly good. We will be just like everyone else who lives with a mindset that never goes beyond the temporal.

Application

» *Think of someone who you can comfort with these words about the second coming of Christ. Let them know that heaven awaits. This life is not heaven; heaven is something we look forward to.*

» *How can you encourage such people that they will not suffer in eternity with whatever they are currently suffering? You do not have to get into debates about eschatology. Christ is coming back, and it could be today.*

19

Encourage and Build up One Another

*"Therefore encourage one another and build one
another up, just as you are doing."*

1 Thessalonians 5:11

EXPLANATION

As noted in the previous section, the same Greek word is
often used for the English translation of "comfort" and
"encourage." "Here the more general sense of 'encourage one
another' rather than the specific sense of 'comfort one another' is indicated by the context."[15]

In 1 Thessalonians 5:11, the context deals with those who
are dead in Christ, and with the coming of the Lord. Paul
states that believers should encourage and build up one another during such uncertain times. They were to come alongside one another and help one another. These acts of encouraging were not to be sporadic, but rather, continuous. This
is what God requires of believers today as well. People can
often become discouraged when they lose sight of what God
will do. They become discouraged when they lack trust in

God's Word. Believers are called to keep others from defeat and despair. When believers are discouraged, other believers must seek to encourage them and build them up.

Believers should seek to encourage with the Word of God. The Greek word for encourage (1 Thessalonians 5:11) is also translated "exhort" in Titus 1:9. Hebrews 3:13 ("But *exhort* one another every day, as long as it is called 'today,' that none of you may be hardened by the deceitfulness of sin.") and Hebrews 10:25 ("not neglecting to meet together, as is the habit of some, but *encouraging* one another, and all the more as you see the Day drawing near") both have a sense of urgency in their use of the term encourage. "The total body is edified only as each member of it experiences growth."[16] As believers encourage one another, they are building up the body of Christ.

ILLUSTRATION

In Acts 4, mention is made of a man named Joseph who was such an encourager that people renamed him Barnabas which means "Son of Encouragement." He encouraged John Mark, the apostle Paul, and anyone else he ran into. He had such a effect on people that his name was changed to more adequately describe him!

APPLICATION

» *List several ways in which others have encouraged you. What was so encouraging about these actions or events?*

» 1.

» 2.

» 3.

» Write down the name of a person you have recently encouraged. State exactly what you did or said by way of encouragement. How did your encouragement contribute to the building up of the body of Christ?

» Pray that you will develop a special friendship. The Puritans used the quaint term, a "Bosom Friend" for someone who was a brother or sister of the same gender as you and who would really encourage you to growth in your faith. Perhaps you could submit a few questions to your friend and ask that friend to ask you those questions on a regular basis so that you could develop accountability with each other.

» Paul teaches in Ephesians 4:29 that we should edify even in our speech. Recall the three most recent conversations you had with another believer. How did you (or did you not) encourage the other person in your speech? What do you need to change to be in alignment with God's Word?

» 1.

» 2.

» 3.

20

Be at Peace with One Another

"And to esteem them very highly in love because of their work. Be at peace among yourselves."

1 Thessalonians 5:13

EXPLANATION

Jesus gives ultimate peace. For a believer, there is peace in one's relationship with God the Father through Jesus Christ. In John 14:27, Jesus says, "Peace I leave with you; my peace I give to you. Not as the world gives do I give to you." If Jesus gives believers peace, what might have been the problem in 1 Thessalonians 5:13 that prompted Paul to say, "Be at peace among yourselves"?

Apparently there was a problem in the church at Thessalonica with the people's view of leadership. In the previous verse, 1 Thessalonians 5:12, Paul told the Thessalonians to appreciate (esteem) their leaders because they were diligently laboring among them. Some people in the church apparently did not understand or appreciate what the leaders were doing. In fact, some may have been complaining about their leaders and criticizing them, not unlike many in churches today. Therefore, Paul directed them to live at peace with one another. This was not a command just for the non-leaders of the church, and neither was it a command just for church leaders—rather, it was a command to all parties involved. Everyone was to take heed to this command.

Robert Thomas writes, "There had to be peaceful relations. Leaders were to guard against abusing their authority; idlers were not to disregard those over them in the Lord."[17] If there was no peace, there would be no unity, and there would be no oneness in Christ. To continue, 1 Thessalonians 5:14 even gives instruction on how one should deal with different types of people in order to achieve peace ("And we urge you, brothers, admonish the idle, encourage the fainthearted, help the weak, be patient with them all"). And verse 15 speaks even more about how to maintain the peace ("See that no one repays anyone evil for evil, but always seek to do good to one another and to everyone").

Scripture is clear in directing how leaders are to behave (Titus 1:6-9; 1 Timothy 3:1-7). They are to..."Shepherd the flock of God that is among you, exercising oversight, not under compulsion, but willingly, as God would have you; not for shameful gain, but eagerly" (1 Peter 5:2) Scripture is also clear on how members of the body are to treat their leaders: "Obey your leaders and submit to them, for they are keeping watch over your souls, as those who will have to give an account. Let them do this with joy and not with groaning, for that would be of no advantage to you" (Hebrews 13:17).

All believers today should live at peace with one another. Whether or not a leader, one should have a Christlike attitude in all relationships.

ILLUSTRATION

Do you appreciate your church leaders? If so you are probably contributing greatly to being at peace with one another. If not, there is likely a lack of unity and peace. Now leaders ought not to abuse their authority—the apostle Peter admonishes them not to be domineering over those under their charge (1 Peter 5:3). If they will love and serve their people and the people will respect and appreciate the leaders, there will be peace with one another. Colossians 3:15 well states that the peace of Christ is to rule in the hearts of believers.

APPLICATION

» *Are you obeying Hebrews 13:17, "Obey your leaders and submit to them, for they are keeping watch over your souls, as those who will have to give an account. Let them do this with joy and not with groaning, for that would be of no advantage to you"?*

» *Who are your spiritual leaders? Are you living at peace with them? If not, explain why this is so and what you might need to do to live at peace with them.*

» *If you are a leader, read Acts 20:17-38 and compare your attitude to that of Paul. Make a note of the specific steps for improvement that might need to be taken.*

» *Are you living at peace with all men? Romans 12:18 states: "If possible, so far as it depends on you, live peaceably with all." Others may not* seek peace with you, but you should seek peace with them, for you are clearly directed to do so, "so far as it depends on you."

» Are there any sins to confess concerning the lack of seeking peace with others? Think of believers with whom you need to more actively seek peace. What steps will you take this week to do that?

21

Seek Good for One Another

"See that no one repays anyone evil for evil, but always seek to do good to one another and to everyone."

1 Thessalonians 5:15

EXPLANATION

In 1 Thessalonians 5:15, Paul uses the present tense to show that seeking after good for one another person should not be a temporary or sporadic action, but rather should be ongoing. The word "seek" indicates pursuing something. There is an active involvement, not an apathetic indifference. There is a hunt to do good. In other words, believers are eager to seek after the good of one another.

This passage is slightly different from the other "one another" commands because believers not only seek after good for other believers (one another), but also for unbelievers (all men) as well. It is most natural and easy to seek after one's own good. It is also easy to seek good for one's own family. Beyond that, it becomes more and more difficult. A believer's responsibility is to do good to others even when good feelings are not present.

Believers must eagerly seek after good for one another and for all men. In 1 Corinthians 14:1 we are directed to pursue love, and Romans 13:10 says that love does no wrong to a neighbor. Thus, loving others is not only putting aside wrongdoing but it is, in fact, actively pursuing the doing of good.

ILLUSTRATION

A pastor and another person went out to lunch during a Bible conference. After they had finished lunch, the pastor went to pay the bill but was told the bill had already been paid. Already paid? At first the pastor thought his colleague had paid but the waitress said a gentleman across the room had paid for it. When the pastor went to thank the gentleman, he said, "I'm also at the conference and I saw that you took this other guy to lunch to minister to him and so I just wanted to do good." This man was on the hunt to do good and he still continues to do these kinds of things—and so, like him, we should always be wanting to do good for one another, actively looking for ways to do so.

APPLICATION

» *How can one seek to do good for one another—
and also for people who are outside of the
Christian faith? Maybe it is as simple as buying
someone a cup of coffee. Perhaps you can offer
to mow a neighbor's lawn or walk her dog.
How about bringing dinner to her home or
inviting her over for dinner? If not dinner, how*

about dessert? Doing good does not need to cost much time or money. But it does require thoughtfulness and care.

» *Make a list of the three most recent things you have done to pursue good for others.*

» 1.

» 2.

» 3.

» *Write down the names of three believers for whom you can seek to do good. What specifically will you do and why?*

» 1.

» 2.

» 3.

22

Pray for One Another

"First of all, then, I urge that supplications, prayers, intercessions, and thanksgivings be made for all people."

1 Timothy 2:1

EXPLANATION

Although this passage does not have the phrase "one another" in it, it does show an important responsibility that believers have toward one another. James 5:16 specifically states that believers are to pray for one another: "Therefore, confess your sins to one another and pray for one another, that you may be healed. The prayer of a righteous person has great power as it is working." What the apostle James wrote, and the relationship between confession and prayer, will be examined more closely later in this book. For now, the focus will be on simply praying for one another.

In 1 Timothy 1:20, Paul mentions two blasphemers of God, Hymenaeus and Alexander, who may have been leaders, and were a negative influence. In this context Paul tells Timothy that various prayers should be made on behalf of all men. Praying for all people is good in God's sight (1 Timothy 2:3) because it is God's desire that all men be saved (1 Timothy 2:4). God wants believers to pray, specifically here for the unbelieving world. Believers must humble themselves before God and seek his mercy upon the lost people in their midst. Hendriksen and others comment about the four words for prayer used here in verse 1. "Entreaties" can also be called "supplications." By using this term, Paul "petitions for the fulfillment of certain definite needs which are keenly felt. [He is] fully aware of his complete dependence on God."[18] This is a request that only God can fulfill. The term "prayers" is a more general, generic term meaning just that—prayer. "Petition" or "intercession" has the idea of "'falling in with,' 'meeting with in order to converse freely'...'in the interest of others.'"[19] This is the type of prayer that is for other people and their needs. The last term used, "thanksgiving," is simply "expressed gratitude."[20]

Believers today also need to be keenly aware of the needs around them in this world and pray to God to show his saving grace. The believer's desire must align itself with God's desire, namely, that all men be saved and "come to the knowledge of the truth" (1 Timothy 2:4).

ILLUSTRATION

David was a freshman in college and was a believer. He met Adam, who was a junior and was an unbeliever. David realized he only had two years before Adam would graduate from college, so he really wanted to share the gospel with him. David wrote down Adam's name on an index card and started praying weekly, and sometimes daily, for his salvation. David sought opportunities to befriend Adam and eventually they got to be good friends. By God's grace, Adam came to saving faith fifteen months after David first started praying for him.

A year after Adam came to faith, David shared with Adam his prayer index card with Adam's name on it. Adam was so encouraged to know that David had been praying for him for all those months that he decided he, too, would do the same for another unbeliever.

Application

» *If you don't have a prayer journal or notebook, start one today. In a notebook, spreadsheet or electronic document, jot down the date you entered the prayer request on the left margin or column. Use the large center column to write down the prayer request. Then use the right margin or column to write the date the prayer was answered. You can keep a running list, or you can use separate pages or tabs for different categories. For example, you can have a separate page or tab for family members, church members, coworkers, non believers, missionaries, sports teammates, classmates, etc.*

» *Churches and/or leaders can also populate their calendars with names of members on each day of the year, and keep repeating the names throughout the year. Larger churches can pray for several members each day and smaller churches can pray for their members multiple times a month or year. The key is to have an easy-to-follow system so you can be sure to pray for one another.*

23

Stir up One Another

"And let us consider how to stir up one another to love and good works."

Hebrews 10:24

EXPLANATION

One Christian author writes, "The reality of Christian love should be demonstrated in the *personal relationships and mutual concerns* of the Christian community" (emphasis added).[21] Hebrews 10:24 shows one practical way these kinds of relationships are possible. In order to properly understand verse 24, one also has to read verse 25, thus: "And let us consider how to stir up one another to love and good works, not neglecting to meet together, as is the habit of some, but encouraging one another, and all the more as you see the Day drawing near." Christians are called to gather together because this is the place of mutual encouragement. It's very important for the saints to gather together regularly—especially as they see the day of the Lord drawing near.

Verse 24 shows how the practical concern of believers for one another distinguishes them as a community from others around them—something that unbelievers do not have. But what does the writer mean when he uses the term "stir up"? Another New Testament passage that uses the same Greek word gives some insight. Acts 15:39 records: "And there arose a *sharp disagreement*, so that they separated from each other. Barnabas took Mark with him and sailed away to Cyprus." The Hebrews 10:24 word "stimulate" is translated "sharp disagreement" in Acts 15:39. The connection may seem strange, but the understanding of its impact for Hebrews 10:24 is significant. In essence, this word means *stimulate, sharp disagreement, irritation*. It is used in a negative way in Acts and in a positive way in Hebrews. There was a *negative provocation* between Paul and Barnabas in Acts, and there should be a *positive provocation* among believers according to Hebrews. It is the same word and has the same meaning, but used in a very different context with very different implications. Believers are, in a sense, to "provoke" other believers to love and good deeds. A cognate form of the word is used in 1 Corinthians 13:5—"[love] is not provoked." We can say that love does not negatively provoke people, but believers are to positively provoke or stimulate one another to love and good deeds. Stimulating is not a passive, "feel good" kind of activity. To stimulate a fellow believer is a conscious and intense action. There is nothing passive about it.

Believers are to stimulate others to love and good works. As the old saying goes, we are to be "a burr under their saddle." Good works are the tangible expressions of care and love and is expected of all believers (Ephesians 2:10). Christians need to be catalysts to stimulate one another to love and good deeds in their lives.

ILLUSTRATION

If you are asked if you can take a meal over to someone who is home from a recent visit to hospital and you cannot do it, you could simply say you are sorry and have to decline. However, you could take it a step further, saying that though you cannot do it that night, you could do it another night. Do not just shut the opportunity down. The person who asked you to take dinner over is trying to stir up in you good works and love for others.

Here is another example: Say there are some prayer requests for someone going through a rough time, but you noticed there was no follow up or help being given. Prayer requests on a white board or in a bulletin are a good start but they fall so short of what this "one another" is about. You can be a catalyst by seeking to meet needs yourself or asking others how they would like to help. This "one another" command really gets down to where we live and it deals with our selfishness. It is all about how we are to love, give, and serve—even when we are tired.

APPLICATION

» *How do you "positively provoke" or "stimulate" others to love and good works? In what ways are you a "catalyst" for others?*

» *Write down the names of some people who appear to be on the periphery of your church. How might you minster to them?*

» 1.

» 2.

» 3.

» *Do you invite this stimulation into your life and give thanks to others when they do it to you? If others are trying to be a catalyst in your life, don't deprive them of their opportunity to practice this "one another" command.*

24

Do Not Speak against One Another

"Do not speak evil against one another, brothers. The one who speaks against a brother or judges his brother, speaks evil against the law and judges the law. But if you judge the law, you are not a doer of the law but a judge."

James 4:11

EXPLANATION

Earlier in James (chapter 3), the author addressed the mighty power of the tongue. Here, he returns to the subject and relates how the sin of speaking against (that is, slandering) one another is related to the sin of judging one another.

To slander means to speak evil, and this is sin. Paul, in Romans 1:30, makes the point that a slanderer is depraved and without excuse. He includes it in the same list as "...haters of God, insolent, haughty, boastful, inventors of evil, disobedient to parents" (v. 30). The underlying Greek word here for speaking against refers to "mindless, thoughtless, careless, critical, derogatory, untrue speech directed against others."[22] How easy it is for one believer to speak against another believer.

There are usually two forms of speaking against people: gossip and slander. Malice is the attitude of the heart that lies behind both. Remember Ephesians 4:31? "Let all bitterness and wrath and anger and clamor and slander be put away from you, along with all malice." Malice is included in the list of characteristics to be put off. It means you have to put off the desire for someone to be harmed—and that is what underlies speaking against one another.

Slander is speaking evil with the addition of lies. Whatever is said in slander is not totally true. This is where we get the word "blaspheme." Gossip, on the other hand, is the way that we speak against others by speaking what may well be true about them behind their back in order to hurt them. The content of what is discussed is not something that should be talked about to anyone else, but we do—and we do it behind their backs out of a desire to puff ourselves up or with the malicious intention hurt them.

In Matthew 12:36, Jesus says, "I tell you, on the day of judgment people will give account for every careless word they speak." This is sobering. It is so easy to make a passing comment about another believer, yet if it does not edify (Ephesians 4:29), we are sinning, and we are speaking against the other person. As James has already mentioned, the tongue is powerful and difficult to control—so it is vitally important for believers to use their speech for good and not for evil. Whether to make a humorous quip or to find acceptance in the crowd, believers must stop the habit of speaking against one another.

ILLUSTRATION

At times you might hear someone say to you (or to another person, who is not part of the problem or solution), "Have you heard about 'so and so'..." or "We need to pray for 'so and so'..." Then they proceed to speak critically about, gossip, or slander the individual. If we are talking about another person and it's not about their good or for their good, what is our motive? Often people will speak the truth about another believer out of malice—that is, it is intending to hurt such a person—and this is gossip. Or, they might say things about another person that are mostly true but add some extra data that makes the report untrue—and this is slander.

APPLICATION

» *In the past twenty-four hours, how have you spoken evil of others? What has motivated you to do this? List the reasons here, then confess them and repent of them.*

» *1.*

» *2.*

» *3.*

» *Read Ephesians 4:15-32 and note the "Four Principles of Communication" listed in the next point. Memorize this and meditate upon it. Seek to implement this into your life immediately. Note where you are failing in this area, then confess and repent of your sin.*

» *Be honest with others as fellow Christians (v. 25); When provoked to anger, don't sin and, if you do, confess and keep current (vv. 26-27); Don't tear people down with your words but build each other up (vv. 29-30); Respond to others like Jesus and not in a fleshly manner (vv. 31-32).*

25

Do Not Grumble against One Another

"Do not grumble against one another, brothers, so that you may not be judged; behold, the Judge is standing at the door."

James 5:9

EXPLANATION

Murmur, complain, grumble, grudge. Many popular Bible translations use one of these words in James 5:9. These words will be used synonymously here. James is not speaking about complaining to another person; rather, he is talking about complaining against another brother. This complaining person is finding fault with, blaming, or blame shifting. In essence, to complain against one another is to blame one another for any wrong you are enduring. This is, in fact, judging him or her. "Groaning and grumbling is the opposite of being joyful and thankful...He sins because he accuses God, perhaps indirectly, for the misfortunes he receives."[23] Ultimately, one who complains against others is blaming God and is guilty of sin.

Keep in mind that if another believer has sinned against you and perhaps some difficult or harmful situation occurred because of that person's actions, then you may apply Matthew 18:15ff and resolve the situation. However, this command to not grumble against one another is not talking about a situation where someone has sinned against you but, rather, is considering a situation where you just want to blame someone for something when that person is not at fault.

Instead of having this sinful attitude, a believer should remember the words of James 1:2: "Consider it all joy, my brothers, when you meet trials of various kinds." This person should pray what the psalmist wrote in Psalm 141:3: "Set a guard, O LORD, over my mouth; keep watch over the door of my lips!" It is important in our pursuit of God-honoring relationships that we should not complain and become embittered against one another.

ILLUSTRATION

Jesus made the point that we should take the log out of our own eye before we try to take the speck out of someone else's eye. It's easy to see ourselves in a better light than the other person. Imagine the following statement: "Yes, I did something wrong *because* she..." This is a common statement we might say or hear where one person is blaming the other person for the conflict. This is complaining against another person rather than taking ownership of our own actions or attitudes ("the log") and being thankful. You only have to read Genesis 3 to see Adam doing this against God and against Eve.

» *List some difficult trials that have come your way recently.*

» *1.*

» *2.*

» *3.*

» *For each of the above trials, note how you responded. Did you blame someone else for this? For example, if you sinned by being angry, did you blame the other person for provoking you to anger? The way for you to deal with that person's provocation is a separate issue. This "one another" command makes the point that you must not blame the person who provoked you, as your sin of anger was your decision. Confess and repent as necessary.*

» *1.*

» *2.*

» *3.*

26

Confess to One Another

"Therefore, confess your sins to one another and pray for one another, that you may be healed. The prayer of a righteous person has great power as it is working."

James 5:16

EXPLANATION

In order to understand this "one another" command more thoroughly, one must look to the preceding and subsequent verses. James 5:14–16 reads as follows:

> Is anyone among you sick? Let him call for the elders of the church, and let them pray over him, anointing him with oil in the name of the Lord. And the prayer of faith will save the one who is sick, and the Lord will raise him up. And if he has committed sins, he will be forgiven. Therefore, confess your sins to one another and pray for one another, that you may be healed. The prayer of a righteous person has great power as it is working.

There is some debate about whether this passage is talking about physical healing being related to confession and prayer, and that is beyond our scope here, but we do know that Scripture is clear that there may be physical consequences arising from sin. David writes, "For when I kept silent, my bones wasted away through my groaning all day long" (Psalm 32:3). However, sickness may not be the result of a person's particular sin. Jesus' disciples asked him, "...'Rabbi, who sinned, this man or his parents, that he was born blind?' Jesus answered, 'It was not that this man sinned, or his parents, but that the works of God might be displayed in him'" (John 9:2-3).

The important point James makes is that one should first confess his sin to God, then to others if and when it is beneficial to the hearers. He is not referring to going to a priest and seeking forgiveness, and neither is he talking about confessing to others without confessing to God. Moreover, James is also not telling his readers to confess a particular sin to every person they might meet. Rather, his point is that the person who sinned should go to the person who has been affected by the sin—and this should be for the sake of restoring their relationship.

To confess means "to be in agreement with." If one confesses, he is agreeing with God that he has violated God's law. Thus, God is always involved with your confession because any sin is always a sin against God. From there, you confess to one another. The purpose of confession to one another is not for catharsis—that is, just to get something out of your system. Confession is to be for the benefit of the one hearing. Edmond Hiebert is right when he says, "The mutual confession must give stimulus and direction to the mutual intercession."[24] One's confession should give way to prayer.

Jay Adams says, "It is important to seek forgiveness when confessing rather than apologizing."[25] Adams also gives some helpful suggestions on how to confess to one another.

* Avoid highly connotative language. Use factual

terms and be as brief as possible. Proverbs 10:19 says, "When there are many words, transgression is unavoidable, But he who restrains his lips is wise" (NASB).

* Don't destroy good words by bad attitudes. Proverbs 25:11, "A word fitly spoken is like apples of gold in a setting of silver." Confession should be done for the right reason.

* Guard against ruining a confession by describing the other person's own sin accusingly. For example, don't say, "Forgive me for saying that when you pulled that dirty trick on me." Look out for the "but you, too" attitudes.

* Don't attach excuses to confession. For example, don't say, "Even though the pressures were great, I guess I shouldn't have done that."[26]

Always keep in mind that confession is first and foremost to God (1 John 1:9) and only then to others.

ILLUSTRATION

It is important to remember that sin committed only in your mind (where no words or actions resulted from this) only needs to be confessed to God. Think of concentric circles where the most inner circle relates to you and God. The next circle includes you and the individual you sinned against. The outermost circle includes you and all others you sinned against.

For example, if a man started lusting after a woman who was singing in the choir, he should not go to her and confess his sin of lust. His sin was not against her as it was all in his mind; it was against God. He should only confess the matter to God and stay within the first inner circle. Confessing his sin her would serve no purpose and would, in fact, hinder her worship as she would now feel extremely awkward singing in the choir, knowing that someone was having sinful thoughts about her.

Similarly, if Jane had jealous thoughts about Carol, Jane should not "confess" to Carol that she had such thoughts; she should simply stay in that innermost circle, confess the matter to God, and seek biblical means to achieve self-control and right thinking. There is no reason for Carol to know of Jane's thoughts. Now, if the jealousy resulted in certain sinful actions, then Jane should confess to the Lord—that is, the inner circle in the illustration—and then to Carol (that is, the next outer circle) because Jane's heart sin has resulted in external, sinful actions against Carol.

Application

» *Examine your heart and see if there are any unconfessed sins you have harbored in your heart (e.g., jealousy, anger, envy, etc.). If so, confess them to the Lord from the perspective of these being in the inner circle.*

» *If these sins have resulted in words to others or external actions, list these unconfessed sins you have committed against other believers. Confess these to the Lord and repent of them. Write out exactly how you will go about confessing these to the people you may have offended and seek their forgiveness (outer circle).*

» *You may find the example of the prodigal son (Luke 15:17-19) helpful in seeing how he practiced what he was going to say to his father whom he had sinned against.*

27

Be Hospitable to One Another

"Show hospitably to one another without grumbling."

1 Peter 4:9

EXPLANATION

This is an interesting command. Hospitality is a specific requirement of an elder (1 Timothy 3:2; Titus 1:8) and a widow who will be placed on the "list" (1 Timothy 5:10). Here, in 1 Peter 4, we see it is also a requirement for all believers. But the term for hospitality in this verse is often misunderstood. Literally, it means "lover of strangers." Believers are called to be lovers of strangers! What a foreign concept to the twenty-first century American way!

Two thousand years ago, hospitality was very different. The "love of strangers" was extremely important to the early church as it facilitated the spread of the gospel. There were travelers such as letter carriers, pastors, teachers, etc., who relied upon the hospitality of other believers so they could help spread the gospel. Hotels of those days were not the same as today. "It was undesirable to lodge in public inns, which were often the scene of drunkenness and impurity; the Christian's faith had cut him off from the pagan practices that generally prevailed there."[27] "It was even more important for believers to find refuge in Christian homes whenever they were fleeing from their persecutors."[28] In 3 John 5-6, we see how one bears witness to love in extending hospitality to other believers.

The first-century believers even practiced hospitality by holding church services in their homes. Romans 16:5 and 1 Corinthians 16:19 testify to this fact, revealing that some graciously opened their homes to other believers for a time of corporate worship (Philemon 2). This may seem unusual to us but "for the first two hundred years there were no separate church buildings."[29] It was commonplace to have meetings at a believer's home for church. Imagine hosting church at your home week after week! Hebrews 13:2 states, "Do not neglect to show hospitality to strangers, for thereby some have entertained angels unawares."

Sadly, not all Christians are known for "Christian hospitality." Why do believers lack this? We will mention a few reasons here as suggestions.

* For some, it may simply be ignorance of God's command and a lack of example of this in their lives. Some believers just never knew that Scripture requires every believer to be hospitable to one another.
* A lack of hospitality may also stem from a lack of genuine love for one another.
* Others may not be hospitable because they are too focused on spending precious time and resources on themselves or these resources are already overcommitted.

While there may be many more reasons for the lack of Christian hospitality, few boil down to adequate reasons.

God's Word commands hospitality, and we, as Christians, should joyfully obey it.

In 1 Peter 4:9 there is a little word at the end of the verse—"without grumbling." People who show hospitality should do so with the right heart and attitude. It doesn't mean much to extend hospitality but then complain the entire time guests are in the home or when they leave. Keep in mind that the recipient of the hospitality may not be able to repay in any way (Luke 14:14). Your attitude—that is, without complaint—is an extremely important part of obeying this command. Let us not forget the words of Jesus quoted by Paul in Acts 20:35, "It is more blessed to give than to receive."

ILLUSTRATION

If it helps you, put down "Hospitality Time" on your family calendar for next Sunday. This way, everyone in your house knows that on Sunday night you are going to have someone over. You can cook or you can order in. You can make it fancy or make it a crockpot meal. If having people over after church, turn on the crockpot before church and everything will be ready when you return. Be sure to invite people you don't know well, perhaps a recent newcomer to church. After all, hospitality means being a lover of strangers. If you do not plan it, hospitality may not take place—so mark your calendar now.

» When were the last three times you were hospitable? What exactly did you do?

» 1.

» 2.

» 3.

» Perhaps you know of some missionaries or other people in ministry who will be in town. Make plans to have them stay at your home, a friend's home, or put them up at a local hotel. Even today, we need to show our love to traveling Christians and so keep the Lord's command.

» "Biblically, historically, and practically, hospitality involves a home."[30] How about hosting a game night next weekend? Board games or video games? Maybe you could host a small casual tea for a new visitor and a few current members?

» Hospitality can also happen outside the home. When was the last time you took someone out for a meal? How about a quick time of fellowship at a local coffee shop? Take a new visitor out to the driving range and fellowship while hitting some golf balls together. In what other practical ways can you show hospitality in today's culture? List them, and then be sure to post them to your calendar.

» 1.

» 2.

» 3.

» *When you travel, are you a good guest? Keep in mind an old saying, "Guests, like fish, begin to smell after three days." Be sure you do not overstay your welcome. Also, keep in mind that, whether you are the visitor or the host, you are there to serve, not to be served (Mark 10:45).*

» *For further consideration, read Alexander Strauch's "The Hospitality Commands."*

28

Serve One Another

---

*"As each has received a gift, use it to serve one
another, as good stewards of God's varied grace."*

1 Peter 4:10

EXPLANATION

The teaching of 1 Peter 4:10 is not a foreign concept in
Scripture. Similar statements are made in Galatians 5:13
("For you were called to freedom, brothers. Only do not use
your freedom as an opportunity for the flesh, but through
love serve one another"), Romans 12:6-8, 1 Corinthians 12,
especially verse 7 ("To each is given the manifestation of the
Spirit for the common good"), and Ephesians 4:12 ("To equip
the saints for the work of ministry..."). God has given every
believer a spiritual gift. The use of this gift is not for one's
own edification—a point clearly made by 1 Corinthians 14:12:
"So with yourselves, since you are eager for manifestations
of the Spirit, strive to excel in building up the church." This
means that all believers should use whatever spiritual gifts
they have in order to serve other believers.

Christians are merely stewards of God. God has given them both spiritual gifts and worldly possessions. All these things must be used for the benefit of the church—i.e., their fellow believers. The point is, every person is a steward and so must make sure he uses whatever he has according to the owner's wishes. For a believer, it means that gifts and other possessions must be used to serve others. One author writes, "The entrustment was not made to him for his own enjoyment; he was responsible to use his gift for the benefit of those he served."[31]

John 13 gives a great example of how believers may serve one another. It was the custom of that time that a servant would wash the feet of guests when they entered the home. However, on this particular evening, Jesus and his disciples were reclining for dinner, but no one washed their feet. Since they were used to this custom of having their feet washed, the disciples knew full well that their feet were not washed. All of a sudden, Jesus took his outer garment off and started washing the disciples' feet (John 13:5). What a shock to those present! Later that evening, Jesus said, "For I have given you an example, that you also should do just as I have done to you" (John 13:15).

Serving one another is easy when the "service" is prestigious or attracts the applause of an audience. Serving one another becomes more real when it is hidden from the view of others. Jesus said, "Beware of practicing your righteousness before men to be noticed by them; otherwise you have no reward with your Father who is in heaven" (Matthew 6:1).

A Bible teacher has made these points about spiritual gifts.

* You will enjoy using your gift. You can always improve in it and get better skilled at it, but you will enjoy what God has gifted you to do.
* Others recognize it. God's people will say you are made for that and should be doing that.
* God seems to bless it.

So you will enjoy it, others will recognize it, and God seems to bless it.

One must begin serving other believers in order to find out where they are gifted in the Body of Christ rather than just taking man-made tests on spiritual gifts. Often, God's people will have their own heart struggles (e.g., fear of man, love of attention, etc.,) that can skew the results of these tests. Spiritually mature saints should have input on guiding the younger believers to explore where they might be gifted as they serve in the Body of Christ in different ways.

Around the time I was taking tests on giftedness, I had not really served in church. (Well, I did serve in the music area at church in college, just by playing the organ or piano, but I found myself wondering if that was where I was gifted to serve the body of Christ especially as, at the time, it was because there was no one else to do it.) When I took the tests to evaluate where my gifts lay, I was asked a set of standard questions like whether I enjoyed speaking in front of other people (absolutely not!) or whether I looked for opportunities to speak (again, absolutely not!). The tests concluded that I did not have speaking gifts— but the tests also did not factor some things in—matters like sin, pride, and selfishness, all of which were in my heart—and which may have prevented me from exercising my calling. The fear of man was behind my answers. I had to acknowledge my fear of man and repent of it. I am very thankful for godly mentors in my life, as well as my wife, who have all helped me to be aware of and confirm my spiritual giftedness.

APPLICATION

» *What do you believe are your spiritual gifts? Speak to your leaders and close friends and see if they affirm what you believe is so.*

» *When was the last time you served others with your spiritual gifts? What did you do? Was it of benefit others or only to you? How was it of benefit the other person? How was it of benefit to the church? Were you serving only to be noticed by others?*

» *Are you serving in ways that others would not serve? Are you doing the less desired tasks? Would you even be willing to clean toilets at your church every Saturday morning if that was a need? List three tasks that can be done for the church or for another believer that you deem to be not very desirable.*

» *1.*

» *2.*

» *3.*

» *Keep in mind that your serving is an act of worship to God (Colossians 3:22-24; 1 Corinthians 10:31). Serving one another is a way of serving God.*

29

Be Humble toward One Another

"Likewise, you who are younger, be subject to the elders. Clothe yourselves, all of you, with humility toward one another, for 'God opposes the proud but gives grace to the humble.'"

1 Peter 5:5

EXPLANATION

Chapter 5 of 1 Peter refers to leaders and their responsibilities to the flock. Leaders are to eagerly shepherd those under them, exercise oversight, not be fond of sordid gain (v. 2), not lord it over others, and be an example (v. 3). These leaders were to be undershepherds of Jesus Christ (v. 4). It is in this context that Peter writes, "Clothe yourselves, all of you, with humility toward one another..." Why would he write this? As Peter tells elders what they need to do, he also tells younger men to be subject to the elders (v. 5a). Immediately after that statement, he writes that they should all be humble toward one another. Elders have a lot of responsibility and visibility and thus can become prideful (cf. 1 Timothy 3:6). Younger men might resent that they have less authority, and they, too, could become prideful. In this context, Peter tells them all that they should be humble. He is not addressing his remarks to only one group of people, but to all the people.

Edmond Hiebert makes this very interesting statement:

> "The humility" or "lowly-mindedness" should characterize their personal relations. The term does not involve an attitude of self-disparagement or servility, but willingness to assume a lowly position to serve others. It is the opposite of self-exaltation, which is the very essence of sin. Such an attitude of humility is a distinctly Christian virtue. Trench notes that the very word "is itself a fruit of the Gospel; no Greek writer employed it before the Christian era, nor, apart from the influence of Christian writers, after."[32]

Perhaps the best picture of humility is seen in Jesus Christ in his incarnation. Philippians 2:8 most graphically depicts this image, "...he humbled himself by becoming obedient to the point of death, even death on a cross."

ILLUSTRATION

When Peter states, "clothe yourselves," he may very well have been thinking of Jesus' example at the last supper when he placed a towel around his waist to wash the disciples' feet. As Jesus girded himself with humility, believers too must do the same toward one another. Having true humility is such a difficult thing. Would a typical modern-day believer have acted like a slave and washed another's feet if he were in the upper room that night? Most likely not! But this is exactly what Jesus requires of believers today. A believer needs to be willing to be a slave to others so he can serve them. Believers need to put off pride and to put on humility.

» *Write down the last three acts you performed for others that you consider to be reflective of a humble servant. When did these events occur?*

» *1.*

» *2.*

» *3.*

» *Are you a leader in the church? Are you a younger person in the church who needs to subject himself to the authority of others? What does this passage in 1 Peter 5:5 say is your responsibility toward others?*

» *For further reading, see Stuart Scott's "From Pride to Humility" (Focus Publishers, 2000, Bemidji; MN). It has a helpful inventory for manifestations of pride and humility that one can take or use.*

30

Greet One Another

"Greet one another with the kiss of love. Peace to all of you who are in Christ."

1 Peter 5:14

EXPLANATION

Consider this short conversation, one that you will likely overhear quite often: "Hi. How are you?" "Fine, thanks. How are you?" "Good, thanks."

Today's greetings has are often little more than a ritual. The "Nice meeting you" and "How are you?" mean little more than "I acknowledge you." There does not seem to be much meaning in today's familiar greetings. Unfortunately, this is true in the Christian arena as well. Christian greetings are no longer different from the greetings of this world. Greetings for believers need more depth and intimacy. God does not require small talk. He requires a genuine greeting of brotherly love.

The "one another" command in 1 Peter 5:14 is repeated at least four other times in the New Testament (Romans 16:16;

1 Corinthians 16:20; 2 Corinthians 13:12; 1 Thessalonians 5:26). Each of these passages mentions a "holy kiss." What is this holy kiss? In essence, kissing is a demonstration of intimacy, and the adjective "holy" is an expression of sanctification. Gene A. Getz rewords it as "Greet one another with pure motives."[33] This is what believers are to do today. In Hiebert's words, "The attitude of the heart should evoke the external act."[34] Today's believers need to imitate the terms in Romans 16, the longest greeting list in Scripture.[35] Note the following intimate terms from Romans 16: *servant, helper, my beloved, outstanding, approved, kinsman, choice man,* and *brethren*. Believers today also need to show affection in their greetings to one another.

ILLUSTRATION

There are some cultural issues that may need considering in dealing with in this passage. Hiebert states, "It should be noted that the apostle did not originate that form of greeting; the custom already prevailed."[36] He also adds, "Kissing as a ritual in the Western church disappeared almost completely by the end of the thirteenth century."[37] So, what should believers today do? It is best to adapt accordingly.

For example, most Christian men in the United States do not kiss each other; likewise, most cultures in the Far East do not promote kissing as a form of greeting. Instead, some cultures show love and respect by individuals shaking hands with both hands—and this can be accompanied by bowing at the waist. Even though the specifics of this "one another" command—kissing—might not apply, the general principle does still apply. Whichever persons we see, we should greet them in a loving, respectful fashion. And we are to do this with a peaceful spirit.

Application

»   *In Luke 11:43 it is recorded that Jesus said, "Woe to you Pharisees! For you love the best seat in the synagogues and greetings in the marketplaces." Does this passage apply to you? Do you seek to be greeted or do you seek to greet others?*

»   *Make a list of those whom you have been neglecting to greet recently. What is the reason for this? If there is any sin involved, confess and repent of it now.*

»   *1.*

»   *2.*

»   *3.*

31

Have Fellowship with One Another

---

*"But if we walk in the light, as he is in the light, we
have fellowship with one another, and the blood of
Jesus his Son cleanses us from all sin."*

1 John 1:7

EXPLANATION

What is fellowship? This is what some have said: "to have
in common,"[38] "joint ownership"[39] "partnership."[40]
These terms sound nothing like most coffee-and-donut
times in many modern churches. The term today is used very
loosely. Fellowship has become a time of merely eating or
a time where people of similar culture or racial background
gather in one room.[41] One author correctly writes, "Christian
fellowship is not the sentimental and superficial attachment
of a random collection of individuals, but the profoundly
mutual relationship of those who remain 'in Christ,' and
therefore belong to each other."[42]

When true fellowship is happening, one's fellowship with
Jesus Christ will be very evident. If believers are walking

closely with God, they will then necessarily walk closely with other believers. Yet, there are many people today who do not really have fellowship with other believers. As I.Howard Marshall stated, "Persons who cut themselves off from fellowship with other Christians cannot have fellowship with God."[43] Even a cursory reading of 1 John will make this point obvious. By walking in the light and having a right relationship[44] with God, one necessarily has fellowship with God the Father. Unity and the profound sense of mutual relationship with the Father will result in unity and biblical relationships with other believers.

Even though this is a separate "one another" command, the command to fellowship with one another can be thought of as the culmination of all the "one another" commands. When the thirty-four other "one another" commands are being practiced as God commanded, true fellowship is necessarily happening. The best way to describe what biblical fellowship looks like is the execution of the other "one another" commands.

ILLUSTRATION

Some people say, "Come on over and fellowship with us," or "We are going to have a church fellowship next Sunday after church." When Christians say these things, do we use the term properly? We often don't think in terms of what the word means or how it is used in God's Word. Maybe it's time to reeducate one another on the true meaning and use of it.

APPLICATION

» *List below some ways you had fellowship this week.*

» *1.*

» *2.*

» *3.*

» *From the list above, which of the other "one another" commands were put into practice? There will likely be multiple "one another' commands.*

» *Are there sins in your life that hinder you from fellowshipping with others? If so, confess and repent of them and seek change in your life. Cf. 1 John 1:6.*

And Just Before We Conclude...

W e have reached the end of the list of thirty-one ways, but there are some additional "one another" passages that we would like to share with you. Consider the next four as a series of bonus readings which we are including in an appendix under the headings A, B, C, and D.

Do Not Deprive One Another

"Do not deprive one another, except perhaps by agreement for a limited time, that you may devote yourselves to prayer; but then come together again, so that Satan may not tempt you because of your lack of self-control."

1 Corinthians 7:5

EXPLANATION

This passage is talking about failing to fulfill your marital duties to your spouse—a command only applicable to married couples. The verb "deprive" basically means to defraud, steal, or rob. The sexual relationship is an important aspect of marriage. Because it is so important in marriage, some use it as a bargaining tool or weapon against the other marriage partner. As discerning believers may guess, such use of sex is clearly unbiblical. Sexually satisfying one's spouse is not an optional event in a marriage relationship, but rather a requirement. The verses preceding 1 Corinthians 7:5 make it abundantly clear that each marriage partner has a "duty" to the spouse in the area of sexual relations. One writer says, "The requirement of continuing sexual relations in marriage is emphasized in terms of a mutual payment of debt."[45] We each owe it to the other and it is not something which should be withheld.

The only exception to regular physical relations in marriage should only be by mutual agreement, for a limited time, and for the purpose of prayer. Biblical counselor, Jay Adams, states that any other reason for withholding sexual intercourse in marriage is sin.[46] Have you ever thought that withholding sex from your spouse is sinning? Paul's teaching in 1 Corinthians 7:5 makes it clear it is. Adams continues to clarify his statement and says that legal separation is also unbiblical for this reason as well, since being apart would lead to depriving one another.[47] Once the brief time of withholding sexual relations due to prayer has ceased, marriage partners should continue in regular sexual relations.

ILLUSTRATION

You may say you are not intentionally withholding. However, you are not intentionally giving. And this "one another" command involves intentional giving. You cannot justify your abstinence with excuses such as "I've been so busy," or "I have so much to do for church," or "The kids have so much going on," etc. You are to be especially careful in this area, so you do not neglect physical closeness and intimacy. This is a command given to you from the Lord. When there is a pattern of coming together sexually and it is interrupted, there is a significant place for temptation. Each couple determines mutually what "regular" frequency in marital intimacy looks like for them and they should seek further godly counsel if necessary.

APPLICATION

» *If you are married, do you have regular sexual relations with your spouse? Does Scripture condone or condemn your actions? If the latter, repent, and confess your sin to God and your spouse.*

» *Discussing sexual relations may be difficult even in a marriage relationship. The resources listed below may be helpful.*

* Mack, Wayne A. *Strengthening Your Marriage.* 2d ed. Phillipsburg, NJ: P&R Publishing, 1999.
* Peace, Martha. *The Excellent Wife: A Biblical Perspective*, rev ed. Bemidji, MN: Focus Publishing, Inc., 1999.
* Wheat, Ed and Gaye. *Intended for Pleasure.* 3d ed. Grand Rapids: Fleming H. Revell, 1997; reprint, 2001.
* Wheat, Ed. and Gloria Okes Perkins. *Love Life for Every Married Couple.* Grand Rapids: Zondervan Publishing House, 1980.
* Scott, Stuart. *The Exemplary Husband.* Bemidji, MN: Focus Publishing, Inc., 2000.

B

Wait for One Another

"So then, my brothers, when you come together to eat, wait for one another."

1 Corinthians 11:33

From Paul's letter, it is evident that the Corinthians had a problem when they came together for the Lord's Supper. Communion during the first century was not like communion in most churches today. Churches of the first century gathered together and celebrated communion as part of their meals. Paul says that people were coming to the communion table seeking to be filled with food instead of seeking to reflect upon the work of Christ on the cross. Thus, those partaking of communion were not loving one another by waiting for fellow believers. Rather, they were seeking to first fill their own bellies and meet their own needs. In Simon J. Kistemaker's words, "When they come together for Communion, the Corinthians must realize that the intent is to receive spiritual rather than physical nourishment."[48] Paul's writing illustrates that people in the Corinthian church did not demonstrate Christian love and care but were self-centered and concerned only with their physical hunger.

Most Christian churches today do not have elaborate

meals and feasts as part of holy communion. Therefore, the probability of a person going to church hungry to gorge on communion wafers is slim. However, believers today can take the principles from this "one another" command to wait on one another. Christians today can have an attitude of seeking the other person's needs before their own. They can seek to be patient and others focused rather than showing the sinful tendency to be self-centered. When the Corinthians came together to eat and celebrate the Lord's Supper, they preferred self over others. Today's Christians should prefer others over self, regarding others as more important than themselves (Philippians 2:3).

ILLUSTRATION

Although the primary meaning of this "one another" command may not be literally applicable today, the principle of the command certainly can be. For example, you can allow others to go first in a lunch line at church or you can give the seat of honor at the table to another instead of taking it for yourself (see James 2:3). If there are only five pieces of meat in an entrée but there are six people present, you can forgo your portion so that others can enjoy the entrée. Holding the door open for someone or allowing another person to exit the elevator first are examples of how the principle of the command can be applied today.

In our busy lives where we are always in a rush, as a form of obedience to this command consider allowing others to go first. Have you ever seen couples walking where the husband is in such a hurry that he is three feet in front of his wife, hoping maybe if he walks faster, she will catch up. Sometimes, the driver gets into the car and starts backing up before the spouse even properly gets in. The scene might even be comical if it were not out of character with biblical values.

The specific applications of this principle today are countless. As you practice the other "one another" commands of Scripture, you will be obeying the command to "wait for one another."

Application

» *List specific ways that you have failed to wait for others at church functions. Confess and repent of these and describe in detail how you will take immediate steps toward change. Really think hard, then try filling out all five spots below. We often are not aware of our own sin and we need to slow down to consider it.*

» 1.

» 2.

» 3.

» 4.

» 5.

C

Consider One Another

*"Do nothing from selfish ambition or conceit, but in
humility count others more significant
than yourselves."*

Philippians 2:3

EXPLANATION

In order to properly understand this command to "count others more significant than yourselves" or put another way, "regard one another," one must understand that the context of Philippians chapter 2 shows the condescension and humiliation of Christ, where he voluntarily waived the rights and privileges of deity, and took upon himself humanity. If God incarnate did this for man, should not believers do likewise for one another? This is exactly what "consider one another" means when Paul writes, "Have this attitude in yourselves which was also in Christ Jesus" (Philippians 2:5).

Often believers get the wrong idea that they must think of themselves in lesser terms than others, or in some sense inferior to others. However, this is not a biblical assessment of self or of others. Scripture does not teach that believers should demean and neglect themselves; rather, it clearly teaches that individuals should have a right view of themselves (Romans 12:3, "...I say to everyone among you not to think of himself more highly than he ought to think, but to think with sober judgment...") and a right view of others (Philippians 2:3, "...in humility count others more significant than yourselves"). Instead of being consumed with self, believers should be preoccupied with the needs of others—above their own needs.

ILLUSTRATION

This command goes so radically against our flesh. When you greet people, you want them to say, "How's it going with *you*? What's going on in *your* life? Tell me about *you*." We are naturally selfish. That is why keeping in step with the Spirit in humility is so important. The Holy Spirit wants to assist us and will help us to take an interest in one another. Pay special attention and give particular effort to thinking of others, caring for them, and deferring to their preferences and interests.

» *List three recent conversations you have had this week. How were you talking more about yourself than consciously trying to regard the other person as more important than yourself?*

» *1.*

» *2.*

» *3.*

» *List three people and, for each individual, write down practical ways you can regard him or her as more important than yourself. Be specific and use actual examples.*

» *1.*

» *2.*

» *3.*

D

Do Not Lie to One Another

---

*"Do not lie to one another, seeing that you have put
off the old self with its practices."*

Colossians 3:9

EXPLANATION

Proverbs 6:16-19 states, "There are six things that the LORD hates, seven that are an abomination to him: haughty eyes, a lying tongue, and hands that shed innocent blood, a heart that devises wicked plans, feet that make haste to run to evil, a false witness who breathes out lies, and one who sows discord among brothers." Among this list of "abominations" to God is "lying." This is a strong term denoting something detestable and offensive. If God considers lying in terms such as these, so, too, should believers who have been washed clean by the blood of the Lamb! It is natural for unbelievers to lie. The devil is described as the "father of lies" (John 8:44), but the Holy Spirit is known as the Spirit of truth (John 14:16-17). Since the Holy Spirit dwells in the hearts of believers, believers are not to have the "habit of lying."[49]

Relationships are built on trustworthiness and truth. If you do not have these two qualities, you do not really have much of a relationship with anybody. When our kids were growing up, we told them that, no matter what they did or did not do, they were not to lie. We needed to be able to trust them and they needed to be able to trust us. It was our rule that if they lied, they would be disciplined more strictly. We really wanted to make the point that if we could not trust them, our relationship was hindered.

There were a few times when they did lie and they refused to own up to it. When we found out they were lying, they were given more severe discipline. If they messed up and did something wrong and were honest about it, of course there was grace for that. In those cases, we would say, "We hope you learn from that." We chose not to add any more discipline because they had learned from what they had sowed and reaped.

APPLICATION

» *What were the last three lies you told? Why did you lie? For each lie, what was the truth you should have told?*

» *1.*

» *2.*

» *3.*

» *Is there a situation in which you are currently lying or intend to lie? If so, explain how you can tell the truth in that situation.*

» *Do you find that you lie to others to be nice or to not hurt their feelings? If so, consider how you can speak to them without lying.*

Conclusion

I n summary, these "one another" commands are a great
challenge to all believers—young and old, mature in the
faith, and young in the faith. We are all in desperate need of
God's grace and help to live these out in light of the gospel
truths of Christ. Many believers may find that they fall short
in one or more of these commands. This is a good realization.
As a person looks to the mirror of God's Word, he should
walk away with conviction and determination to change and
become more obedient.

Perhaps you are beginning to realize that you are struggling in one or more of these "one another" commands in
your relationship with other believers. Perhaps this is a good
time for you to reflect upon your relationship with Jesus
Christ and see if you are in the faith. Or maybe you find that
you are having a hard time with most of these commands
with a particular person in your life—so perhaps this is the
time to commit yourself to obeying these commands, especially with other believers in mind.

It may be that you have realized from reading this that
you lack a conscious desire to pursue a truly *biblical* relationship with others. What you may have found out is that
you need to actively seek to practice the "one another" commands in your life. Most believers do not seem to be intentionally disobedient, especially in regard to relationships,
but what can happen is that you are not *actively* seeking to
implement the commands of Scripture into your daily life in
a habitual fashion. So, why not seek to consciously implement these commands with your spouse, parents, children,
friends, elders, etc.? And remember, these commands should
even be applied to strangers! There are no qualifying statements to these "one another" commands. Pray about each
of the thirty-five "one another" commands we have consid-
ered. You could pray about one or two of these each day of

the month—a great way to help you consciously be aware of these commands and your need to seek God-honoring relationships with others.

We pray that as you practice the one another commands, you will start to see a marked change in your relationship with your family and your church. "For it is God who is at work in you, both to will and to work for His good pleasure" (Philippians 2:13). To God be the glory!

Bibliography

Adams, Jay E. *A Theology of Christian Counseling*. Grand Rapids: Zondervan Publishing House, 1979.

--------. *Competent to Counsel*. Grand Rapids: Zondervan Publishing House, 1970.

--------. *From Forgiven to Forgiving*. Amityville, NY: Calvary Press, 1994.

--------. *I Corinthians, II Corinthians* in *The Christian Counselor's Commentary*. Hackettstown, NJ: Timeless Texts, 1994.

Bruce, F. F. *1 & 2 Thessalonians* in *Word Biblical Commentary*, eds. David A. Hubbard and Glenn W. Barker. Waco, TX: Word Books, 1982.

Crotts, John. *Graciousness: Tempering Truth with Love*. Grand Rapids, MI: Reformation Heritage Books, 2018.

Getz, Gene A. *Building Up One Another*. Wheaton, IL: Victor Books, 1976. Reprint, 1978.

--------. *Encouraging One Another*. Wheaton, IL: Victor Books, 1981.

--------. *Loving One Another*. Wheaton, IL: Victor Books, 1979. Reprint, 1983.

--------. *Praying For One Another*. Wheaton, IL: Victor Books, 1982.

--------. *Serving One Another*. Wheaton, IL: Victor Books, 1984.

Harrison, Everett F. "Romans" in *The Expositor's Bible Commentary*, ed. Frank E. Gaebelein, Vol. 10. Grand Rapids: Zondervan Publishing House, 1976.

Hendriksen, William. *The New Testament Commentary, Galatians*. Grand Rapids: Baker Book House, 1968. Reprint, 1974.

--------. *The New Testament Commentary, I & II Timothy and*

Titus. Grand Rapids: Baker Book House, 1957.

--------. *The New Testament Commentary, I & II Thessalonians*. Grand Rapids: Baker Book House, 1955. Reprint, 1975.

--------. *The New Testament Commentary, Romans*. Grand Rapids: Baker Book House, 1980. Reprint, 1995.

Hiebert, D. Edmond. *1 Peter*, rev. ed. Chicago: Moody Press, 1992.

--------. *James*. Chicago: The Moody Bible Institute, 1979. Reprint, Winona Lake, IN: BMH Books, 1997.

--------. *The Epistles of John*. Greenville, SC: Bob Jones University Press, 1991.

Hughes, Philip Edgcumbe. *A Commentary on the Epistle to the Hebrews*. Grand Rapids: William B. Eerdmans Publishing Company, 1977.

Kistemaker, Simon J. *The New Testament Commentary, Exposition of the First Epistle to the Corinthians*. Grand Rapids: Baker Book House, 1993.

--------. *The New Testament Commentary, Exposition of the Epistle of James and the Epistles of John*. Grand Rapids: Baker Book House, 1986.

Lane, Timothy S., and Paul David Tripp. *Relationships: A Mess Worth Making*. Greensboro, NC: New Growth Press, 2008.

Lenski, R. C. H. *The Interpretation of St. Paul's Epistle to the Romans*. Minneapolis: Lutheran Book Concern, 1936. Reprint, Minneapolis: Augsburg Publishing House, 1961.

Mack, Wayne A. *Maximum Impact: Living and Loving for God's Glory*. Phillipsburg, NJ: P&R Publishing, 2010.

--------. *Strengthening Your Marriage*. 2d ed. Phillipsburg, NJ: P&R Publishing, 1999.

MacArthur, John. *Biblical Parenting for Life, Teacher's Manual*. Sun Valley, CA: Grace Community Church, 2000.

--------. *1 Corinthians* in *The MacArthur New Testament Commentary*. Chicago: Moody Press, 1984.

--------. *Galatians* in *The MacArthur New Testament Commentary*. Chicago: Moody Press, 1987.

--------. *James* in *The MacArthur New Testament Commentary*. Chicago: Moody Press, 1998.

Marshall, I. Howard. *The Epistles of John* in *The New International Commentary on the New Testament*, ed. F. F. Bruce. Grand Rapids: Wm. B. Eerdmans Publishing Co., 1978.

Moo, Douglas. *The Epistle to the Romans* in *The New International Commentary on the New Testament*, ed. Gordon D. Fee. Grand Rapids: Wm. B. Eerdmans Publishing Co., 1996.

Murray, John. *The Epistle to the Romans* Vol. 2, in *The New International Commentary on the New Testament*, ed. F. F. Bruce. Grand Rapids: Wm. B. Eerdmans Publishing Co., 1965.

Orr, William F., and James Arthur Walther. *I Corinthians* in *The Anchor Bible*, ed. William F. Albright and David N. Freedman. Garden City, NY: Doubleday & Company, Inc., 1976.

Peace, Martha. *The Excellent Wife: A Biblical Perspective*, rev. ed. Bemidji, MN: Focus Publishing, Inc., 1999.

Phillips, Jim. *One Another*. Nashville: Broadman Press, 1981.

Robertson, A. T. *A. T. Robertson's Word Pictures in the Greek New Testament*, 1934 in *BibleWorks CD 3.5*, 1996.

Sanday, William, and Authur Headlam. *A Critical and Exegetical Commentary on the Epistle to the Romans*, 2d ed. Edinburgh: T & T Clark, 1962.

Scott, Stuart. *From Pride to Humility: A Biblical Perspective*. Bemidji, MN: Focus Publishing, Inc., 2002.

--------. *The Exemplary Husband*. Bemidji, MN: Focus Publishing, Inc., 2000.

Smalley, Stephen S. *1, 2, 3 John* in *Word Biblical Commentary*, eds. David A. Hubbard and Glenn W. Barker. Waco, TX: Word Books, 1984.

Strauch, Alexander. *The Hospitality Commands: Building Loving Christian Community: Building Bridges to Friends and Neighbors*. Colorado Springs, CO: Lewis & Roth Publishers, 1993.

Thomas, Robert L. "1 Thessalonians" in *The Expositor's Bible Commentary*, ed. Frank E. Gaebelein, Vol. 11. Grand Rapids: Zondervan Publishing House, 1978.

Welch, Ed T. *Caring for One Another*. Wheaton, IL: Crossway, 2018.

Wheat, Ed, and Gaye Wheat. *Intended for Pleasure*. 3d ed. Grand Rapids: Fleming H. Revell, 1997; Reprint, 2001.

Wheat, Ed, and Gloria Okes Perkins. *Love Life for Every Married Couple*. Grand Rapids: Zondervan Publishing House, 1980.

About Stuart Scott

Stuart Scott teaches in the graduate program of Biblical Counseling at The Master's University in Santa Clarita, CA. He has over forty years of experience in counseling and pastoral ministry. He is a Fellow with the Association of Certified Biblical Counselors. Stuart is an author as well and he and his wife, Zondra, have two grown children and two grandchildren. His academic credentials and associations include the following:

Professor of Biblical Counseling, The Master's University, Santa Clarita, CA;
Director of Membership Services, the Association of Certified Biblical Counselors (ACBC)
Director of One-Eighty Counseling and Education, Louisville, KY and Santa Clarita, CA
Adjunct Professor of Biblical Counseling, Southern Seminary, Louisville, KY

BA, Columbia International University, Columbia, SC
M.Div, Grace Theological Seminary, Winona Lake, IN
ThM, Southern Theological Seminary, Louisville, KY
DMin, Covenant Theological Seminary, Saint Louis, MO

About S. Andrew Jin

S. Andrew Jin (B.S, University of Virginia; M. Div., The Master's Seminary, M.A. Biblical Counseling, The Master's University) grew up in Fairfax, Virginia but now calls Los Angeles his home with his wife, Esther, and their children, Hope, Abigail, and Caleb. He is a Director at an alternative investments firm in West Los Angeles. He is also the author of a chapter in *Men Counseling Men: A Biblical Guide to the Major Issues Men Face* (Dr. John D. Street, General Editor) and is a member of the Association of Certified Biblical Counselors.

About Shepherd Press

Shepherd Press Publications are...

○ Gospel driven
○ Heart focused
○ Life changing

Our invitation to you

We passionately believe that what we are publishing can be of benefit to you, your family, your friends, and your work colleagues. So we are inviting you to join our online mailing list so that we may reach out to you with news about our latest and forthcoming publications, and with special offers.

Visit:

www.shepherdpress.com/newsletter

and provide your name and email address.

For more information about this imprint, visit

www.shepherdpress.com/store/counsel-for-the-heart/

Endnotes

1 William Sanday and Arthur Headlam, *A Critical and Exegetical Commentary on the Epistle to the Romans*, 2d ed. (Edinburgh: T & T Clark, 1962), 361.

2 Ibid., 783.

3 Everett F. Harrison, "Romans" in *The Expositor's Bible Commentary*, ed. Frank E. Gaebelein, Vol. 10 (Grand Rapids: Zondervan Publishing House, 1976), 134.

4 John Murray, *The Epistle to the Romans* Vol. 2, in *The New International Commentary on the New Testament*, ed. F. F. Bruce (Grand Rapids: Wm. B. Eerdmans Publishing Co., 1965), 137.

5 Douglas Moo. *The Epistle to the Romans* in *The New International Commentary on the New Testament*, ed. Gordon D. Fee (Grand Rapids: Wm. B. Eerdmans Publishing Co., 1996), 874.

6 Simon J. Kistemaker, *The New Testament Commentary, Exposition of the First Epistle to the Corinthians* (Grand Rapids: Baker Book House, 1993), 186.

7 Jay Adams, *From Forgiven to Forgiving* (Amityville, NY: Calvary Press, 1994), 82.

8 A. T. Robertson, *A. T. Robertson's Word Pictures in the Greek New Testament*, 1934, in BibleWorks CD 3.5, 1996 on Colossians 3:18.

9 Technically this is for slaves and masters, not employees and employers. But a point of application would be that you must keep a submissive attitude to your employer if you wish to stay at that place of work.

10 Jay Adams, *Competent to Counsel* (Grand Rapids: Zondervan Publishing House, 1970), 44.

11 Adams, 49.

12 William Hendriksen, *The New Testament Commentary, I*

& *II Thessalonians* (Grand Rapids: Baker Book House, 1955; reprint, 1975), 91.

13 For further reading and application, consider *Maximum Impact: Living and Loving for God's Glory* by Wayne A. Mack, P&R Publishing.

14 Jim Phillips, *One Another* (Nashville: Broadman Press, 1981), 50-51.

15 F. F. Bruce, *1 & 2 Thessalonians* in *Word Biblical Commentary*, eds. David A. Hubbard and Glenn W. Barker, (Waco, TX: Word Books, 1982), 115.

16 Robert L. Thomas, "1 Thessalonians" in *The Expositor's Bible Commentary*, ed. Frank E. Gaebelein, Vol. 11 (Grand Rapids: Zondervan Publishing House, 1978), 287.

17 Ibid., 288.

18 William Hendriksen, *The New Testament Commentary, I & II Timothy and Titus* (Grand Rapids: Baker Book House, 1957), 91.

19 Ibid., 92.

20 Ibid., 93.

21 Philip Edgcumbe Hughes, *A Commentary on the Epistle to the Hebrews* (Grand Rapids: William B. Eerdmans Publishing Company, 1977), 415.

22 John MacArthur, *James* in *The MacArthur New Testament Commentary* (Chicago: Moody Press, 1998), 221.

23 Kistemaker, *Corinthians*, 166.

24 D. Edmond Hiebert, *James* (Chicago: The Moody Bible Institute, 1979; reprint, Winona Lake, IN: BMH Books, 1997), 299.

25 Jay E. Adams, *A Theology of Christian Counseling* (Grand Rapids: Zondervan Publishing House, 1979), 221.

26 Ibid.

27 D. Edmond Hiebert, *I Peter*, rev. ed. (Chicago: Moody Press, 1992), 273.

28 Ibid., 274.

29 Ibid., 274.

30 Phillips, 90.

31 Hiebert, *I Peter*, 275.

32 Ibid., 310.

33 Gene A. Getz, *Building Up One Another* (Wheaton, IL: Victor Books, 1976. Reprint, 1978) 64.

34 Hiebert, *I Peter*, 331.

35 Phillips, 74.

36 Hiebert, *I Peter*, 331.

37 Ibid.

38 I. Howard Marshall, *The Epistles of John* in *The New International Commentary on the New Testament*, ed. F. F. Bruce (Grand Rapids: Wm. B. Eerdmans Publishing Co., 1978), 104.

39 Stephen S. Smalley, *1, 2, 3 John* in *Word Biblical Commentary*, eds. David A. Hubbard and Glenn W. Barker (Waco, TX: Word Books, 1984), 12.

40 Ibid., 12.

41 James Hiebert, *The Epistles of John* (Greenville, SC: Bob Jones University Press, 1991), 46.

42 Smalley, 12.

43 Marshall, 111-112.

44 Smalley, 12.

45 William Orr and James Arthur Walther, *I Corinthians* in *The Anchor Bible*, ed. William F. Albright and David N. Freedman (Garden City, NY: Doubleday & Company, Inc., 1976), 208.

46 Jay Adams, *I Corinthians, II Corinthians* in *The Christian Counselor's Commentary* (Hackettstown, NJ: Timeless Texts, 1994), 46.

47 Ibid.

48 Kistemaker, *1 Corinthians*, 405.

49 Robertson, Colossians 3:9.